Who are the people of God? Luke's purposes in the Acts of the Apostles are to identify the church, to establish the legitimacy of its gospel and to demonstrate that God was an active force in history. He wanted to show that the communities of Jewish and, increasingly, Gentile Christians are the true heirs of God's promises to Israel. He gives the history of the early church from the last decades of the first century as the communities become separated from their Jewish origins, and Paul plays the lead role. Acts offers an apologetic for the mixed mission of the church: first to the Jews and then to Gentiles who are included in the chosen people. Luke was an eyewitness to some of what he reports, but his authorship and views have been questioned. This is a theological interpretation of the history of the church within history: Luke is an artist, a narrator rather than a systematic theologian, but writes about the roles of God, Christ and the Holy Spirit, and of the church.

NEW TESTAMENT THEOLOGY

General editor: James D.G. Dunn,
Lightfoot Professor of Divinity, University of Durham

THE THEOLOGY OF THE ACTS OF THE APOSTLES

This series provides a programmatic survey of the individual writings of the New Testament. It aims to remedy the deficiency of available published material, which has tended to concentrate on historical, textual, grammatical and literary issues at the expense of the theology, or to lose distinctive emphases of individual writings in systematized studies of 'The Theology of Paul' and the like. New Testament specialists here write at greater length than is usually possible in the introductions to commentaries or as part of other New Testament theologies, and explore the theological themes and issues of their chosen books without being tied to a commentary format, or to a thematic structure drawn from elsewhere. When complete, the series will cover all the New Testament writings, and will thus provide an attractive and timely range of texts around which courses can be developed.

THE THEOLOGY
OF THE
ACTS OF THE APOSTLES

JACOB JERVELL

Emeritus Professor of New Testament Studies,
University of Oslo

CAMBRIDGE
UNIVERSITY PRESS

Published by the Press Syndicate of the University of Cambridge
The Pitt Building, Trumpington Street, Cambridge CB2 1RP
40 West 20th Street, New York, NY 10011–4211, USA
10 Stamford Road, Oakleigh, Melbourne 3166, Australia

© Cambridge University Press 1996

First published 1996

Printed in Great Britain at the University Press, Cambridge

A catalogue record for this book is available from the British Library

Library of Congress cataloguing in publication data

Jervell, Jacob.
The theology of the Acts of the Apostles / Jacob Jervell.
p.   cm. – (New Testament theology)
Includes bibliographical references and index.
ISBN 0 521 41385 0 (hardback). – ISBN 0 521 42447 X (paperback)
1. Bible. N.T. Acts – Theology.
2. Bible. N.T. Acts – Criticism, interpretation, etc.
I. Title. II. Series.
BS2625.5.J47 1996
226.6'06–dc20 95–30484 CIP

ISBN 0 521 41385 0 hardback
ISBN 0 521 42447 X paperback

Contents

Editor's preface

Although the New Testament is usually taught within Departments or Schools or Faculties of Theology/Divinity/ Religion, theological study of the individual New Testament writings is often minimal or at best patchy. The reasons for this are not hard to discern.

For one thing, the traditional style of studying a New Testament document is by means of straight exegesis, often verse by verse. Theological concerns jostle with interesting historical, textual, grammatical and literary issues, often at the cost of the theological. Such exegesis is usually very time-consuming, so that only one or two key writings can be treated in any depth within a crowded three-year syllabus.

For another, there is a marked lack of suitable textbooks round which courses could be developed. Commentaries are likely to lose theological comment within a mass of other detail in the same way as exegetical lectures. The section on the theology of a document in the Introduction to a commentary is often very brief and may do little more than pick out elements within the writing under a sequence of headings drawn from systematic theology. Excursuses usually deal with only one or two selected topics. Likewise larger works on New Testament Theology usually treat Paul's letters as a whole and, having devoted the great bulk of their space to Jesus, Paul and John, can spare only a few pages for others.

In consequence, there is little incentive on the part of teacher or student to engage with a particular New Testament document, and students have to be content with a general overview, at best complemented by in-depth study of (parts of) two or

three New Testament writings. A serious corollary to this is the
degree to which students are thereby incapacitated in the task
of integrating their New Testament study with the rest of their
Theology or Religion courses, since often they are capable only
of drawing on the general overview or on a sequence of
particular verses treated atomistically. The growing importance
of a literary-critical approach to individual documents simply
highlights the present deficiencies even more. Having been
given little experience in handling individual New Testament
writings as such at a theological level, most students are very ill-
prepared to develop a properly integrated literary and theological response to particular texts. Ordinands too need more
help than they currently receive from textbooks, so that their
preaching from particular passages may be better informed
theologically.

There is need therefore for a series to bridge the gap between
too brief an introduction and too full a commentary where
theological discussion is lost among too many other concerns. It
is our aim to provide such a series. That is, a series where New
Testament specialists are able to write at a greater length on
the theology of individual writings than is usually possible in the
introductions to commentaries or as part of New Testament
Theologies, and to explore the theological themes and issues of
these writings without being tied to a commentary format or to
a thematic structure provided from elsewhere. The volumes
seek both to describe each document's theology and to engage
theologically with it, noting also its canonical context and any
specific influence it may have had on the history of Christian
faith and life. They are directed at those who already have one
or two years of full-time New Testament and theological study
behind them.

University of Durham   JAMES D. G. DUNN

Abbreviations

AASF	*Annales academiae scientiarum Fennicae*
Anch.B	Anchor Bible
Beg.	F.J. Foakes-Jackson, and K. Lake, (eds.) *The Beginnings of Christianity*, Part I: *The Acts of the Apostles* I–V
BETL	Bibliotheca ephemeridum theologicarum lovaniensium
BHTh	Beiträge zur historischen Theologie
BWANT	Beiträge zur Wissenschaft vom Alten und Neuen Testament
BZNW	Beihefte zur Zeitschrift für die neutestamentliche Wissenschaft.
Clem. Al.	Clement of Alexandria
EKK	Evangelisch-Katholischer Kommentar
Ench. Bibl.	*Enchiridion Biblicum*
ET	*Expository Times*
Euseb. *H.E.*	Eusebius, *Ecclesiastical History*
EvTh	*Evangelische Theologie*
EWNT	*Exegetisches Wörterbuch zum Neuen Testament*
FRLANT	Forschungen zur Religion und Literatur des Alten und Neuen Testaments
FS	*Festschrift*
HThK	Herders Theologischer Kommentar zum Neuen Testament
INT	*Interpretation*
Irenaeus *A.H.*	Irenaeus, *Against the Heresies*
JBL	*Journal of Biblical Literature*

xi

JSNTSS	Journal for the Study of the New Testament Supplement Series
KEK	*Kritisch-exegetischer Kommentar über das Neue Testament*, founded by H.A.W. Meyer
LXX	Septuagint (Greek) version of the Old Testament
MS(S)	Manuscript(s)
NTD	Neue Testament Deutsch
NTS	*New Testament Studies*
NTT	New Testament Theology
OT	Old Testament
RB	Revue biblique
RGG	K. Galling (ed.), *Die Religion in Geschichte und Gegenwart*, Tübingen 1957–65
RHPhR	*Revue d'histoire et de philosophie religieuses*
SBL	Society of Biblical Literature
SBLMS	Society of Biblical Literature Monograph Series
SBS	Stuttgarter Bibelstudien
SBT	Studies in Biblical Theology
SN	Studia Neotestamentica
SNTA	Studiorum Novi Testamenti Auxilia
SNTSMS	Society for New Testament Studies Monograph Series
SQE	K. Aland (ed.), *Synopsis Quattuor Evangeliorum*, Stuttgart 1964
StANT	Studien zum Alten und Neuen Testament
StNT	Studien zum Neuen Testament
TDNT	G. Kittel and G. Friedrich (eds.), *Theological Dictionary of the New Testament* Grand Rapids 1964–76
Tertullian, *Adv. Marc.*	Tertullian, *Against Marcion*
ThHK	*Theologisches Handkommentar*
ThLZ	*Theologische Literaturzeitung*
ThWNT	G. Kittel, G. Friedrich (eds.), *Theologisches Wörterbuch zum Neuen Testament*, Stuttgart 1933–
TNTC	Tyndale New Testament Commentary

TRE	*Theologische Realenzyklopädie*
TU	Texte und Untersuchungen
WUNT	Wissenschaftliche Untersuchungen zum Neuen Testament
ZDPV	*Zeitschrift des deutschen Palästina-Vereins*
ZNW	*Zeitschrift für die neutestamentliche Wissenschaft*

CHAPTER I

The author and his sources

No one had undertaken to write down what happened after the resurrection of Jesus and his revealing himself to some of the disciples. Luke had already written a Gospel as he was not completely satisfied with the ones he knew (Luke 1:1–4). He intended to shed more light on what actually happened with Jesus and even give more correct information on the story. But the story of Jesus did not come to an end with his christophanies. The parousia did not come as early as expected. A community had emerged within the boundaries of the old one, Israel. The members of the community were mostly Jews, but with the problem that a growing number of them came from the Gentiles. With the years the community became separated from its origins because of the influx of the Gentiles. Not least did this influx make the question of the law, that is the Mosaic Torah, a burning issue. And the question about the identity of this community arose: who are the Christians? Could this gathering of peoples in more than one community actually be called the people of God? If they were not the people of God, they were nothing. Then also the question of the future of this community arose, for they knew that only the people of God had a future. And this community was not exactly like any other party in Israel. Luke took it upon himself to answer the questions. Various answers had been given by others in the community, but they had not been written down in full or in a sequence. And Luke was not in agreement with some of the answers given so far.

Who was Luke to take upon himself such a task? As do the authors of the other Gospels, he preserves his anonymity, and

does so even in the Acts of the Apostles, but not very success-
fully, as his use of 'we' shows us where he personally took part
in the events (16:10–17; 20:5–15; 21:1–18; 27:1–28:16).[1] He was a
fellow worker and travelling companion of Paul but not one in
the first rank, rather a more insignificant and shadowy person,
one from the backbenches. Luke is known to us, in a historically
reliable tradition from Philemon 24, Colossians 4:14 and
2 Timothy 4:11, as a physician and co-worker of Paul. He is the
only one among Paul's co-workers seen by the tradition as the
author of Acts,[2] an inference which cannot be drawn from the
Gospels. It is the received tradition that has named Luke as the
author. If the idea was to give authority to the writing through
the name of the author, no one would have chosen Luke when
they had far more significant and prominent companions of
Paul at their disposal.[3]

A companion of Paul as the author of Acts? This has always
been questioned in critical exegesis. There are mistakes on
important points in Paul's biography;[4] the charismatic miracle-
worker Paul of Acts is far from the suffering apostle of the
Pauline letters, more like Paul's adversaries than Paul himself;[5]
it is important for Paul to be seen as a legitimate apostle,[6] but
Luke mentions his apostolate only in passing (14:4,14), and not
on the same level as that of the Twelve; the specific theologou-
mena of Paul are there only in a rudimentary fashion in Acts,
e.g. justification by faith (Acts 13:38f.), Christ's expiatory death
(Acts 20:28, cf. Luke 22:20), the law is differently orientated,[7]

---

[1]   For a survey over the various interpretations of the 'we'-passages, see C.J.
       Thornton, *Der Zeuge des Zeugen. Lukas als Historiker der Paulusreisen*, WUNT 56, 1991,
       93–119.
[2]   Irenaeus *A.H.* III, 1.1; 10, 1; 14, 1; 23, 1; the anti-Marcionite Prologue, *SQE* [2] 1964,
       533; the Muratorian canon, *Ench. Bibl.* 3, 35–7. Further: Tertullian, *Adv. Marc.* IV 2,
       2; Origen in Euseb. *H.E.* 6, 25, 6; Euseb. *H.E.* 3, 4.6–7; Clem. Al. in Euseb. *H.E.* 6,
       15, 5; the monarchian Prologue, *SQE* 538f.
[3]   Cf. J.M. Creed, *The Gospel according to St Luke*, London 1930, xiii–xiv; C.J. Thornton,
       Zeuge, 78f.
[4]   Two visits of Paul in Jerusalem before the Apostolic Council (Acts 9:26; 11:30; 15:2);
       different in Paul's writing (Gal. 1:18; 2:1).
[5]   H. Koester, *Introduction to the New Testament*, Philadelphia/Berlin/New York 1982,
       II, 310.
[6]   Gal. 1:1; Rom. 1:1; 1 and 2 Cor 1:1, but not in the other letters.
[7]   J. Jervell, *Luke and the People of God*, Minneapolis 1972, 133–152.

and Luke has other anthropological presuppositions; the important Apostolic Decree (Acts 15:20,29; 21:25) is not mentioned by Paul at all; he asserts that the meeting in Jerusalem made no suggestions to him (Gal. 2:6). Is it possible to connect with Paul the Jewishness of Acts, the concept of the church as Israel, the Jewish life and law observance of the apostles and Paul, the obligations of the Gentiles to the law in the form of the Apostolic Decree? And Luke has not a single quotation from the Pauline letters.[8]

Still Luke must be considered as the author of Acts. We actually have a one-sided account of Paul, based primarily upon his most polemical letters (Rom., Gal. and 1 and 2 Cor.) and so emerges a picture of Paul as the prominent and polemical theologian from the fifties and beginning of the sixties. We overlook that Paul actually was a manifold and complex figure, with obvious tensions,[9] and one whose theology developed and underwent changes in the course of the years, not least in relation to important theological ideas such as law, justification, and the fate of Israel and the Gentiles. Paul is not unambiguous even when dealing with the law.[10] Did his churches and his companions really understand Paul? You can find all Pauline theological conceptions in Acts, even if sometimes in a rudimentary form. And all the concepts of Paul in Acts can be traced to the Pauline letters, but there more in the background and in the shade, without significant theological importance.[11] What we find in Acts is the average, unpolemical theology, which characterizes Paul apart from his most polemical letters in the times of his hardest controversies.

Paul plays the lead in Acts, outshining all other characters, even the twelve apostles. Acts is to a great extent the story of Paul (Acts 9 and 13–28), and Paul has all apostolic prerogatives, being to Luke above all the apostle to the people of God, Israel, and the one who brought the gospel to the whole world (Acts 9

---

[8] This, however, does not prove that Luke did not know the letters, only that he for some reason did not quote from them directly.

[9] Cf. J. Jervell, *The Unknown Paul*, Minneapolis 1984, 52–67.

[10] H. Räisänen, *Paul and the Law*, WUNT 29, Tübingen 1983.

[11] J. Jervell, *Unknown Paul*, 52–67.

and 13–21).[12] Even if he is mentioned as an apostle only in passing (Acts 14:4,14), he is in fact a 'chief apostle'[13] and a leader of the church. All the apostolic prerogatives are bestowed upon him.[14] The christophanies bestow on Paul a unique revelation of the risen Lord (Acts 9, 22 and 26). The geography of Paul's missionary works reveal that Paul is the only apostle to the whole world and fulfils the missionary command of Jesus (Acts 1:8; Luke 24:46). Luke gives us some biographical information concerning Paul which we cannot find in the Pauline letters.[15] It is no wonder that, even so, he presents biographical errors, as these were hard to avoid bearing in mind all the rumours and all the confusion connected with Paul, which forced even Paul himself to correct some of it. And in biographical matters Paul is not always the one who presents the correct version. When it comes to the Apostolic Decree, never mentioned by Paul, Luke is obviously correct: the decree was resolved at the Apostolic Council (Acts 15). But Paul did not see the decree as binding for himself. It is impossible to say if Luke knew any of the Pauline letters; he did not use them, and why should he? As one of Paul's companions he had the best possible information. Luke presents a picture of Paul that to some degree conforms with the ideal of a missionary that Paul's opponents cherished. But Paul himself maintained that he had performed miracles and possessed all charismatic gifts (2 Cor. 11:16ff.; 12:1ff.,11ff.). The point is that Paul not only had more charisma than his opponents, but even his partaking in the sufferings of Christ was a sign of his apostleship.[16]

Luke's main interest is to demonstrate the church as the one and only true Israel, the unbroken continuation of the people of God in the time of Messiah-Jesus. The Christian message

---

[12]   J. Jervell, *Unknown Paul*, 68–76; *People of God*, 153–84.

[13]   Cf. 2 Cor. 11:5.

[14]   J. Jervell, *Unknown Paul*, 52–67.

[15]   Tarsus (9:11, 30; 11:25; 21:39; 22:3); Roman citizen (16:21ff.; 22:25ff.; 26:12); delegate for the High Priest (9:2; 22:5; 26:12); disciple of Gamaliel the Great (22:3; 9:10ff.; 22:12) etc.

[16]   Cf. J. Jervell, 'Der schwache Charismatiker', in *FS für E .Käsemann zum 70. Geburtstag*, Tübingen 1976, 185–98.

cannot be separated from the religious, political and cultural fate of Israel. The Jewishness of Acts, compared to all other New Testament writings, is conspicuous: in the pre-Pauline christology, in the ecclesiology; where the church is Israel; in the soteriology, with the promises of salvation given only to Israel; in the law, the Torah, with its full validity for all Jews in the church; in Paul being the missionary to Israel and the Dispersion.[17] For years scholars were nearly unanimous in viewing Acts as a Gentile-Christian document, written by a Gentile Christian for Gentile Christians. This is not tenable any longer, as it is based to a great extent upon the idea that after 70 AD Jewish Christianity had disappeared, was of no importance, existing only as a marginal feature outside the church. And so no Jewish Christian could have written a book like Acts after 70 AD. But Jewish Christianity was an important and widely spread part of the church throughout the first century.[18] That Luke was able to write Greek in a good style does not show that he was a Gentile – many Jews did so. In spite of his ability to write decent Greek, he does so only seldom and sporadically. Most of his work he presents in what may be called biblical Greek, clearly influenced by the Septuagint, a Jewish book, written for Jews and not for Gentiles. Luke's stylistic home was the synagogue. He was a Jewish Christian. Maybe he was born a Gentile, but then he came from God-fearers, having his roots in a Hellenistic–Jewish Christianity.

When Luke wrote his Gospel he drew attention to his sources (Luke 1:1–4). Even for Acts he had at his disposal various and rich sources. The only one he explicitly announces is Scripture. The Scriptures are the source not only of the history of Israel, but also of the Jesus story and even of the history of the church.[19] Even if we are able to state that he has a number of other sources, it is difficult to determine and separate them.

---

[17] The explanation for these features has been given by the catchword 'history': the Jewish character belongs for Luke to the past, to the first Christian generations. It is not possible to explain Luke in this way, as all the features mentioned are integral parts of the gospel and the church throughout Acts.

[18] J. Jervell, *Unknown Paul*, 26–51.

[19] See the section 'The Scriptures' in chapter three below.

There is, in other words, one clear difference between his use of the Scriptures and his use of other sources; the latter have been thoroughly rewritten by Luke, who has left on them his own stylistic mark. The language of the sources has so become the language of Luke himself.

The very best source was written down by himself as an eyewitness to part of the story he tells, namely the history of Paul and his congregations. There is a wealth of details in the 'we-sections' compared to other parts of Acts, even details with no significance for his account.[20] These details are not explainable as a part of Luke's memory, as Luke wrote Acts about thirty years after his voyages with Paul. We can assume that Luke took notes when the things happened and so could use his own notes years later. For the last section of the story of Paul, his trial (Acts 21–8), Luke had another written source, a report from the lawsuit.[21] It deals above all with court sessions. It is not a court record meant as a defence for Paul and addressed to the Roman authorities. Everything is focused on Paul's biography: the court's decision is never reached. The report is written from a theological point of view and thus full of theological sayings which the Romans could not understand. The report is intended for the Pauline congregations, and contains instruction and exhortation on how to behave towards the authorities, Jewish and Roman. It is a coherent report, not composed of isolated stories, and full of details – that is, it is a written source. Even here Luke rewrote the source, not only with regard to language and style, but by emphasizing the conflict between Paul and the Jews, whereas the Roman authorities are put into the shade. Luke's sources[22] were above all the oral traditions, stemming from the earliest period of the church. The conditions for the formation of a tradition about the apostolic times were favourable.[23] From the beginning a tradition was formed with regard

[20] C.J. Thornton, *Zeuge*, 275ff.

[21] V. Stolle, *Der Zeuge als Angeklagter. Untersuchungen zum Paulusbild der Apostelgeschichte*, BWANT 102, Stuttgart 1973, 260–7.

[22] The theory of a so-called itinerary containing mostly an inventory for missions has met great support, cf. above all M. Dibelius, *Aufsätze zur Apostelgeschichte*, FRLANT 60, Göttingen 1951, 64f., 110, 167ff.

[23] J. Jervell, *People of God*, 19–40.

to the activity of the apostles, other leading figures of the
church, the Jerusalem congregation, and mission.[24] Reports of
the deeds of the apostles and the faith of the congregation had
their place in the life of the church, precisely in the proclamation.[25] The faith and life of a congregation simply served as a
word of God, being proclaimed in the missionary efforts.
Reports about the establishment, the growth and the life of a
congregation have the purpose of furthering missionary work
and of admonishing other congregations. The original model is
the congregation in Jerusalem, which had a special status in the
church.[26] Missionary reports served as recommendations for the
proclamation when new congregations were founded, as confirmation of the gospel for the congregation sending out the
missionaries and as legitimation for the missionaries.[27] Everywhere in the church you could find a remarkable amount of
information about Jerusalem and other congregations.[28] This
was common property, to which naturally Luke had access. This
information was primarily of an oral nature, but not exclusively
so. Letters of recommendation were necessary for the missionaries,[29] and reports about the life and growth of a congregation
even came through letters to and from the missionaries.[30] This
information was to be found even in the synagogues, as the
Jewish Christians remained members of the synagogues as long
as possible. The persecutions of the Christians by the Jews
reported in Acts presuppose a certain knowledge.

Paul's one-time co-worker, Luke, belonged himself to the
second generation. For Paul's missionary work, Luke himself
was the primary source. Obviously, he was with Paul only for a
restricted time, and so he was in need of other sources. He
knew from his own congregation[31] what went on in the church

---

[24] Rom. 1:8; Col. 1:6,25; 1 Thess. 1:6ff.; 3:6; 2 Thess. 3:7ff.; 1 Cor. 4:6,17; 11:1; 2 Cor.
4:7–13; 8:18; Phil. 3:7; 4:9.
[25] 1 Thess. 1:8ff.; 2 Cor. 3:2; Col. 1:4ff.   [26]   1 Thess. 2:14; Rom. 15:25f.
[27] Missionary reports play a great role in Acts: 8:14; 9:27; 11:1,22; 14:26f.; 15:3,7,12;
21:19,21.
[28] Gal. 1:17ff.,23; 2:1ff.,11ff.; 1 Cor. 1:12; 9:3ff.; 2 Cor. 12:11ff., cf. Rom. 15:19.
[29] Cf. 2 Cor. 3:1ff.   [30]   Cf. 1 and 2 Cor.
[31] Probably Antioch, a central and important church where a considerable amount of
information was gathered, as the church here had its origin in Jerusalem and was
very active in its missionary efforts.

in general. And especially regarding Paul there existed a veritable plethora of diverse information – sayings, stories, rumours, accusations, slanders – authentic and inauthentic.[32] In addition Luke had connections with other Pauline co-workers, who gave him necessary information.[33]

A third of the content of Acts consists of speeches. The question of the origin, the sources or the traditions is complicated. German-speaking interpreters commonly regard the speeches as Lucan compositions, so that Luke is the author of the speeches, they are literary in character and were never actually delivered,[34] whereas English-speaking scholars mainly remain unconvinced on this point. Historians in antiquity composed speeches and put them into the mouths of their central figures, thereby interpreting the occurrences for the readers. Luke follows this practice.[35] The speeches in Acts are not verbatim reports. Quite apart from the Lucan language, they are too short to be actual speeches (taking only a couple of minutes to deliver). We have very different types of speeches in Acts constructed in various ways: missionary (2:14–41; 3:11–26; 4:8–12; 5:29–33; 10:34–43; 13:16–41); congregation (1:16–22; 11:5–17; 15:6–11,14–21; 20:16–35); polemic (14:14–18; 17:22–31; 28:17–20; 28:25–8), and apologetic (7:2–53; 22:1–21; 23:1–6; 24:10–21; 26:2–23). Moreover, we have speeches from Jews, Roman officials etc. (5:35–9; 19:25–7,35–40; 24:2–8; 25:24–7). The different types of speeches do not have the same scheme, but even within one group we find different structures. The polemic speeches have nothing in common formally. Neither have the missionary speeches, located as they are in different situations.[36] The only missionary speech by Paul (13:16–41), has some features in common with some of Peter's speeches (e.g. 2:14–36 and 10:34–43), but also significant differences in its

---

32 E. Plümacher, 'Apostelgeschichte', *TRE* III, 1978, 499.
33 Luke probably had information from correspondence (9:2; 22:5; 15:23b-29; 18:27; 23:25ff.; 25:26–7; 28:11).
34 Above all: M. Dibelius, *Aufsätze*, 120–62.
35 M. Dibelius, *Aufsätze*, 120–5; cf. H.J. Cadbury, 'Speeches', *Beg*, V, 402–7.
36 If we should define the speeches in 14:14–18 and 17:16–31 as missionary speeches, for their scheme differs totally from the others. The speech of Peter to Gentiles (10:34–43) has nothing in common with the speeches in Acts 14 and 17.

composition.[37] Luke has in view not only his readers, but also the audience of the given historical situation.

Is it inconceivable that speeches from apostles and missionaries were repeated and kept over the years? Or did the churches take care only of words of Jesus, and not those of apostles? Luke obviously knew something about Paul's speeches, but did the churches take no interest in the speeches from the first generation? The Pauline letters tell us (1.) that Paul's own preaching was preserved from an early stage, being of use for the congregations and as a response to adversaries; (2.) that the proclamation of the apostles and leaders in Jerusalem was universally known in the churches, as this played an important role in the discussion on the Gentile mission and in controversies about Paul, e.g. in the one dealing with the collection. So we actually have a *Sitz im Leben* for the preservation of speeches from the apostles. The letter to the Romans is a 'collection speech' within a letter.[38] Paul's own preaching is being kept (1 Thess. 1:8ff.), where we even find the main features of his proclamation to Gentiles. Paul's sermons are universally known, even that he himself is a part of the content of his preaching (2 Cor. 4:1–6; 1 Cor. 15:8f.; Rom. 15:18ff.). Paul refers to his own preaching, which he has in common with the apostles in Jerusalem (1 Cor. 15:1–11). In Jerusalem he has submitted a report on his teaching (Gal. 1:11; 2:2ff.). His adversaries, even from his own churches, regarded him as opposed to the apostles in Jerusalem, which shows knowledge of the preaching. In 2 Corinthians 10–12 he speaks ironically and polemically about the preaching of 'the super-apostles' (12:11) and others (cf. Rom. 15:20f.; Phil. 1:12ff.). The original gospel came from Jerusalem (Rom. 15:26ff.; 1 Cor. 14:36). In the missionary speeches in Acts the preachers refer to themselves as witnesses (2:32; 3:15; 5:32; 10:39,41; 13:31), and this coincides with what Paul reports of the preaching in the church.[39] So

---

[37] Paul has a historical résumé, 13:17–23, whereas Peter starts with the outpouring of the Spirit and quotation from Scripture.

[38] J. Jervell, 'The Letter to Jerusalem', in K.P. Donfried (ed.), *The Romans Debate*, Minneapolis 1977, 61–74.

[39] J. Jervell, *People of God*, 19–39.

speeches of the earlier preaching are being kept over the years. We even have in the speeches elements from tradition. Sometimes Luke even deals with available speeches or fragments of speeches. Luke's hand in the speeches is clear, as he has rewritten them: this is evident from language and style. Anyway, the speeches give us not only historical information, but also the main theological ideas of Luke.

Luke's style is of great importance for the understanding of the way he presents his theology. Luke is no systematic theologian. He does not give us an account of fundamental conceptions and explicit theological statements. Luke is more of a poet, an artist, a narrator. His style is above all determined by concern to elucidate. He has great skill in composing a narrative, giving us the history of the church by means of pictures, lively, dramatic and broad scenes and fragments of scenes. He employs the style of 'dramatic episodes', known to us from the tragic historians in antiquity. He is not interested in the single episodes as such, but in the continuous historical process – that is, he creates 'aus Geschichten Geschichte',[40] history from stories. His theology is to be found not within, but behind his narrative account, where we have his theological presuppositions.

[40] M. Dibelius, *Aufsätze*, 113.

CHAPTER 2

Purpose and historical setting

We have a series of different theories about Luke's purpose in writing Acts:

A defence for Paul in his trial.

Luke wants to gain the advantages of the status of *religio licita* for the church or to present political apologetic.

Luke wants to clear away misconceptions for Jewish Christians about Paul.

A defence of Paul's memory and his preaching.

A defence against Gnosticism and docetism.

A confirmation of the gospel.

Evangelism.

Acts demonstrates the trustworthiness of the proclamation of Christ.

The promises in the Scriptures and of Jesus are fulfilled in the church.

Luke wants to write the last book of the Bible or continue the biblical history.

Acts gives a *Heilsgeschichte* for the third generation of Christians.

Very often the purpose has been seen in connection with the presentation of Paul. This is legitimate since from Acts 9 onwards Paul is the central figure and seventeen chapters are devoted to him. Three issues must be taken into account in considering Luke's purpose: (1.) the strong Jewish character of Acts; (2.) the interpretation of the Scriptures, and (3.) the position of the law-observant apostle and missionary to the Jews, Paul. The Jewish life of the churches is described in a way that shows it to be self-evident for the readers; the same is true for the interpretation of the Scriptures, whose authority is taken for granted. Far more difficult is the presentation of Paul. Other figures of the church are seen as well known to the readers – Peter, the Twelve, James the brother of the Lord, Barnabas etc., – whereas Luke presents Paul in every detail and his life apologetically, as if he were previously unknown to his readers, but in a way acceptable to them. To Luke the church is 95 per cent a Pauline church, that is, Paul is the founder of 95 per cent of the congregations.[1] Luke turns down the Jewish accusations that Paul had opposed Israel, the law and the temple (21:28; 24:13–16; 26:22f; 28:17), and that therefore the church is not the people of God, and the mission to the Gentiles is not legitimate. Luke is out to demonstrate and guarantee to his readers that the church actually is Israel, that the promises now are being fulfilled and that salvation is given. Paul is above all the guarantee. And Luke will also give his readers 'authentic knowledge about the matters of which [they] have been informed' (Luke 1:4). So he will overcome an insecurity connected with the status of the church.

Luke does not reveal directly who his addressees are. But they are clearly Christians. If Acts is a defence for Paul in his trial, the Roman authorities are the addressees. Some have seen Gentiles in general as the addressees, and if that is the case then Luke had other than Christians in mind.[2] But Acts would be incomprehensible to Gentiles, as Luke presupposes that Christianity is well known to his readers and he gives no introduction to it. Moreover, it is obvious that the Gospel and Acts have the same author. So a main consideration is Luke's elimination of material from Mark and the source Q regarding Jewish ritual purity, and explanations and adjustments of Palestinian traditions to a Hellenistic situation. But all these presumed adjustments, partly of a non-theological sort, occur in the Gospel and not in Acts. Here Luke refers to Jewish terms, titles and customs

---

[1]   Luke passes over whole territories even if he knows about congregations there (Syria, Cilicia). He is only interested in the Pauline territories.

[2]   F.F. Bruce, *The Acts of the Apostles*, Grand Rapids[3] 1990 21–6; H. Köster, *Introduction to the New Testament*, Philadelphia/Berlin/New York 1982, II, 308.

etc. without any kind of explanation.[3] In Acts there are Semit-
isms, Aramaisms, Hebraisms and, above all, Septuagintalisms.[4]
And in Acts Luke is highly interested in those customs about
which it is said he does not care in his Gospel. Luke's elimination
of material dealing with controversies between Jesus and the
Jewish leaders in matters of law (e.g. Mark 7:1–23) does not
prove a Gentile-Christian destination for his writings. Luke
could not possibly picture Jesus as opposed to the Pharisees and
to the law itself, when he expressly defends Jesus against
accusations that he had altered the law (Acts 6:14) and introduces us to the law-observant Pharisee Paul. And so it is more
likely that the elimination of the material in question is deliberate in order to show the position of the law in the church.

The readers are obviously not of a Gentile origin,[5] as we can
see their Jewish origin; it is impossible for anyone without a
Jewish background or firsthand information about Judaism to
understand Luke's presentation. The old, pre-Pauline christology is marked by the fact that the Messiah of Luke–Acts is
the most Jewish Messiah within the New Testament, in regard
not only to terminology, but also to content. Luke employs
some seemingly very old christological titles, going back to the
church in Jerusalem. The messianic title is not simply taken as
tradition, but is explained, reinterpreted and defined precisely
from what can be seen as a Jewish-Christian way of thinking.

As for Luke's conception of the church, the word he uses is
not 'church', *ekklesia*, even if he knows the term, but 'people',
laos, which means Israel as distinguished from all other peoples
and nations. There is for Luke only one Israel, the people of
God *par excellence*. Throughout Acts there are reported repeated
mass conversions of Jews,[6] some mass conversions of God-
fearers,[7] and none of Gentiles. The Scriptures play a dominant

---

[3]   The only exception is Acts 23:8.
[4]   The use of Septuagint in Luke–Acts is no proof of Luke's Gentile audience.
       Hellenistic-Jewish literature is opaque to non-Jews.
[5]   This is the common opinion among scholars, coming from the understanding of
       the history of early Christianity: Jewish Christianity had disappeared after 70 AD.
       Jewish Christians had returned to the synagogue, and became Gentile Christians
       or settled as isolated Christian-Jewish sects.
[6]   2:41; 4:4; 5:14; 6:1,7; 9:42; 12:24; 13:43; 14:1; 17:10ff.; 21:20.
[7]   11:21,24; 13:43; 14:1; 17:4,12; 18:8,10.

role in determining the doctrines of the church. It goes without saying that the Scriptures are in themselves the proof of the legitimacy of the church. They contain the full history of the people of God, and also the history of Jesus and the church. In regard to soteriology, we may note that all promises of salvation are given to Israel; the promises are never removed from the people. Within the church the law, *Torah*, has full validity for all Jewish Christians, and not only as regards ethics, but above all in ritual and sacrificial matters. Even for non-Jews, that is for God-fearers, the law of Moses is valid, as the Apostolic Decree proves. It is not that fulfilling the law gives remission of sins and salvation, but that the people of God keeps the law in order to remain the people of God. Jewish words, conceptions and customs appear throughout Acts, and Luke does not find it necessary to give any explanation. Acts presents us with Paul not as the apostle to the Gentiles, but as the apostle to the Jews and to the world, which is to say the Dispersion. Paul is the Pharisee *par excellence*, not an ex-Pharisee, but, so to speak, the eternal Pharisee. In the lawsuit against Paul (Acts 22–8), the only topic under discussion is the question of law and resurrection, all from a Jewish point of view. When it comes to language, Luke is able to write Greek in a decent style, but most of Acts he presents in biblical Greek, clearly influenced by the Septuagint, which is thoroughly Jewish. More than any other New Testament writer, Luke has to prove whatever he says from the Scriptures, which to him have their proper place in the synagogue. Christianity is the religion of Israel. All these elements clearly point to Christian Jews as the addressees.[8] Acts is designed for internal Christian use.[9] The readers were well acquainted with Christianity and Judaism. Luke's church con-

[8] It is impossible to subsume all the Jewishness of Acts under history, as though it belonged only to the past. Luke maintains that he is writing the history of his own time, and the church, at least in the last part of Acts, is Luke's own church. The time of the apostles is the ideal for the later church, so that history places obligations on the present. The law-observant Paul is a norm.

[9] For the view that Luke also consciously appealed to pagan readership: F.F. Bruce, *Acts*, 21–6; H. Köster, *Introduction to the New Testament* II, 308; A. Loisy, *Les Actes des Apôtres*, Paris 1920, 104–21; J.C. O'Neill, *The Theology of Luke in its Historical Setting*, London ² 1970, 184f.; C.W. van Unnik, 'The "Book of Acts" the Confirmation of the Gospel', *Sparsa Collecta* I, Leiden 1973, 372. This is problematic.

sisted mainly of Jews, as is apparent from the many reports on mass conversions of Jews. The last report with a description of the church's composition, Acts 21:20, gives us 'myriads', thousands and thousands of Torah-abiding Jews; the Jews are innumerable in the church over the whole world. There is another group consisting of 'Jews and God-fearers', Jews and non-Jews, but as one group, because the God-fearers are Gentiles with ties to the synagogue (13:43; 14:1; 17:4,12). Both Jews and Gentiles, that is God-fearers, accept the gospel, but the Jews are greatly in the majority. The conclusion from the reports of mass conversions is confirmed by the description of the Pauline churches. The church as a whole consists mainly of the Pauline congregations, in addition to which there are chiefly the churches in Jerusalem and Antioch. Luke gives us only hints of the expansion of Christianity independent of Paul. The world-wide church outside Palestine, above all in Asia Minor and Greece, is the outcome of Paul's work.[10] The picture is clear; the members of the church are, with some exceptions, Jews; they are Jews with a history, that is, their Jewish history is an inherent part of their life as Christians. There are in addition some Gentiles, who are not members of the people of Israel, but attached to it.[11]

As the church consists mainly of Jews, so too the opposition that the missionary encounters principally comes from the Jews. The persecutions started as early as in the Jerusalem period (4:1ff.; 5:17ff.). The same happened in the Dispersion (13:42f.,45; 14:2ff.; 17:5f.,12; 18:12). There is an interplay between the rejection and acceptance of the gospel by the Jews. Luke sets conversion over against persecution: the persecution comes as an answer to the missionary success of the church. In the chapters devoted to Paul's trial before the Roman authorities (21–8), we are not, as is usually maintained, dealing with a

[10] With the exception of Jerusalem and Antioch all the churches in Acts are founded by Paul. Luke does not mention a church in Rome, only some Christians.

[11] If the members of the church mainly were Gentiles, it would be impossible to explain the reports of mass conversions. Luke wrote Acts about twenty-five years after the death of Paul, and it is simply inconceivable that all those Christian Jews had vanished and that the church consisted only of Gentiles.

political–apologetic aspect, with the Roman authorities as addressees, but with the charges directed against Paul from the Jews (21:21,28; 23:29; 24:5; 25:8,19; 28:17). So even in this part of Acts Luke directs his reader's mind to the 'Jewish question'. This means Luke is not writing in order to convince Jews about the truth of his message, but he is writing to Christian Jews who are under pressure and persecution from their countrymen, in order that they might have 'certainty concerning the doctrines in which [they] have been instructed' (Luke 1:4). The interplay between mass conversions and opposition from the Jews demonstrates that Israel has not rejected the gospel, but has become divided over the issue. The situation for the readers and their adversaries is that both parties claim the heritage of Israel, that is, to be the only people of God.

Luke's readers had their problems with the Jews and so with their own identity and claim on Israel. In the last decades of the first century many Christian Jews left the church and returned to the synagogue. There was obviously a relapse into Judaism. Luke is writing Acts in order to prevent such a relapse. So he had to solve some problems his readers felt to be an obstacle to their claim on the heritage of Israel. There was the problem with the Mosaic law, not being kept by the whole church. Luke demonstrates very clearly that the Jewish Christians, including Paul, were law-observant people. There is no criticism whatsoever of the law in the church. Even the non-Jews in the church keep the law, that is that part of the law required for non-Israelites, the Apostolic Decree. The Gentile mission poses a problem, but not the mission among Jews. Even after 70 AD, Luke makes a rigorous defence of the legitimacy of the mission to the Gentiles. He shows that the God of Israel had forced the church to missionary efforts among non-Jews, showing that the influx of Gentiles into the church is a part of the promises to Israel. And the Gentiles of the church are mostly God-fearers. Paul is a problem to Luke's readers. The problem is the rumours – baseless, according to Luke – concerning Paul's teaching about Israel and the law, as well as his apostasy from Judaism. In a church claiming to be the restored Israel, the law must be fulfilled and the customs of the fathers preserved. If the rumours about Paul are true, the church cannot acknowledge him. So Luke demonstrates Paul as the apostle to the Jews, a Pharisee with a continuing fidelity to the law. And Christianity is true Judaism.

In the last decades of the first century, these problems were acute for large parts of the church, where there were mixed congregations of Jews and Gentiles. Luke is above all dealing with the Pauline missionary areas. But the problem was there even for the church in Jerusalem, as is seen above all from Acts 21. We know from Galatians 2 that the problem existed even in Antioch. And there is not one common solution to the question about the fate of Israel,[12] so that Luke represents his own.

[12] See chapter four, 'Acts and the New Testament'.

CHAPTER 3

The theology of Acts

GOD AND HIS PEOPLE

The Jewish accusations against the church, to which Luke repeatedly refers, have to do with God and the people, Israel. It is alleged that the church has spoken against God and the people (6:11; 21:28; 28:17).[1] These accusations are based upon alleged alterations of the Mosaic law (6:14; 21:21). God is the giver of the law which is a revelation of his will, and to speak against the law, means to speak against God himself and his people. Two groups invoke the same God and claim that they belong to the same people, but one of them denies the other the right to speak about God as their God and Israel as their people. What the church actually is doing, according to the Jewish adversaries, is opposing the God of Israel and writing off the people as the chosen people. That is idolatry. And that is the accusation Luke has to face for his church.

The very centre of Luke's theology is his notion about *God* as the God of Israel. He designates God as the 'God of this people, Israel' (13:17, cf. Luke 1:68; 20:37); 'the God of the [our] fathers' (Acts 3:13; 5:30; 7:32; 22:14; 24:14),[2] the 'fathers' always

---

[1] On several occasions, Luke gives summaries of the charges against Stephen and Paul: Acts 6:11,13,14; 21:21,28; 28:17, see also 24:5; 25:8. The other elements in the charges are: the temple, the law and, once, the emperor.

[2] These Jewish titles are not limited to a certain part of Acts, e.g. to the account of the church in Jerusalem, or used in addressing Jews only, as if Luke wanted to show how the first Christians spoke about God. It is completely inconceivable for him that the later Christians spoke about God in a different way from the first ones, the 'fathers'.

being the Israelite forefathers;[3] 'the God of Abraham, Isaac and Jacob' (3:13; 7:32); 'the God of Jacob' (7:46). Even when Luke designates God as creator, 'maker of heaven and earth and sea and of everything in them' (4:24; 14:15; 17:24), the Jewish content is unmistakable: the designation serves to demonstrate God's power over the enemies, both of the Messiah and of the people (4:24f.); further to condemn and write off idolatry, 'shrines made by men', and to show God's power over history (14:15f.; 17:24). It is remarkable that Luke never uses divine titles in order to show that God is God of the Gentiles, peoples, nations, all, the world etc.[4] And he never defines God from the Christ-event, e.g. as 'the God who raised Jesus from the dead', for the only way to demonstrate the legitimacy of Christ is to link him with the God of Israel, and not the other way round.

God as the God of Israel and his creative power are, above all, demonstrated in his directing the history of Israel. God's history is exclusively his history with Israel. The history of other peoples is not worth mentioning, as their history is an 'empty' one, characterized by God's absence (Acts 14:16). Other peoples are left alone 'to go their own way' (14:16):[5] theirs is a history of idolatry and ignorance (Acts 14 and 17). But in the history of Israel God is continuously active. Therefore Luke offers two detailed representations of the history of Israel (Acts 7:2–53 and 13:16–25). The faithfulness and mercy and patience of God, determined by God's choice of Israel as his only people, are decisive for the history of the people. The beginning of the story is the choice of the fathers (13:17); therefore he exalted the people and brought them out of Egypt (13:17); therefore he bore with them in the desert, gave them a land and appointed judges, prophets and kings for them (13:18–22); therefore he kept his promises to David and brought Israel a saviour, the son of David (13:23–5). This in spite of the sins of the people: they thrust aside the saviours God sent them (7:9,25ff.,35,39); they

---

[3] 3:13,25; 5:30; 7:2,11,12,15,19,32,38,39,44,45,51–3; 13:17,32,36; 15:10; 22:1,14; 26:6; 28:25.

[4] Cf. e.g. Rom. 3:29; 10:12.

[5] This is said only once about the history of Israel: God turned away from the people and gave them over to idolatry (Acts 7:39ff.). That was an act of God, too, and he returned to his people.

even became idolaters (7:39ff.); they misjudged God's being, and built a house for him (7:44ff.); they were stubborn, heathen at heart; they have persecuted the prophets, fought the spirit and have not kept the law (7:51–3). God's answer to this unfaithfulness is repeated new promises to the people and his saving guidance of Israel (7:5–8,10–16,17ff.,33f.,35–8,52). In spite of their idolatry and persecution of the prophets, he sends them new prophets and even the last saviour, the Messiah (7:52). God's power over history is above all expressed through the emphasized and reiterated *dei*:[6] God's will and acts are irresistible, as is expressed at Acts 5:38f. Whatever is of human origin will collapse, whereas it is impossible to put down the work of God. Everything predicted in the Scriptures about Israel, God will fulfil (Acts 1:16; 3:18; 13:27; Luke 1:20; 4:21; 21:24; 22:16; 24:44).

Consequently *the* sin is idolatry, that is, denial of the law and its first commandment (Acts 7:40–3). The outcome of such a denial was the setting up of the golden calf in the desert, so that even Israel, in a central period of its history, turned out to be idolatrous. Luke saw the first commandment to be the very core of the law, and he saw idolatry as ignorance, what happens when you do not recognize God as creator. Then all idols are only products of human hands (7:38ff.; 17:29; 19:26), and so nothing but follies (14:14–18). The seriousness and central place of this sin is seen in the fact that no mission takes place among heathens, as the history of the Gentiles is the history of idolatry (14:14–18; 17:22ff.). The Gentiles admitted to the church are the God-fearers, only these are acceptable to God; of these Cornelius is the paradigm (10:34f., further 10:1ff.,22). And the first prescription in the Apostolic Decree is to abstain from idolatry, 'pollutions of idols' (15:20). When King Herod allows people to hail him as a god he is immediately punished by God with death (12:22–3). That God is the creator, as distinct from men, is stressed in a way that even puts the temple into the shade: it goes without saying that God does not live in shrines, for they are made by men (17:24ff.); God does not accept service at

6   Luke has 40 of the 100 occurrences in the New Testament.

men's hands, for he is himself the giver of life, the creator
(17:25ff.); the shrines belong to the idols. And so not even the
temple in Jerusalem is God's dwelling-place (7:44ff.). The
temple is not a house for God, but a house for the people, a
place to keep the law, only a temporary place for worship.

It is a *conditio sine qua non* to prove that everything in the Jesus-
event and in the church is caused by the God of Israel. This is
stressed by Luke in a way that even thrusts Christ into the
background in Acts. He plays a remarkably passive role compared to that in other New Testament writings. It was the God of
Israel who raised Jesus from the dead. The resurrection is in itself
the fulfilment of the promises to Israel, to David, and it is even
characterized as 'the hope of Israel' and the subject, the core, of
the Jewish prayers and liturgy (2:29ff.; 23:6; 24:15; 26:6f.; 28:20).
It is important to Luke when he deals with the resurrection to
mention God, *theos*, explicitly and to talk about him as having the
only active part in the resurrection[7] ($2:24^8$,30,32ff.,36; 3:15,26;
4:10; 5:30; 10:40; 13:30,33,34,37; 17:31; 24:15; 26:8,23).

The God of Israel is the one who performs the miracles,
those of Jesus and those of the apostles and missionaries (2:22;
4:30). Luke knows about others performing miracles (8:9; 19:13),
and it is important to show that only the God of the people is
responsible for the Christian ones, now performing miracles as
he once did through Moses (7:36). The miracles of Jesus are
only mentioned twice in Acts, but then in a very characteristic
way: God established the identity of Jesus to the people by
means of wonders and signs (2:22; 10:38). Miracles performed
by others are mentioned in some summaries with a stereotypical
and characteristic form: God does signs and wonders through
apostles etc. (2:19; 4:30; 14:3,27; 15:4,12; 19:11) or signs and
wonders occur through them (2:43; 5:12; 8:13; 19:11–12).[9] Even

---

[7]   This is a distinctive feature of Luke, whereas the rest of the New Testament writers
regularly use *egeirō* in aor. passive, in a few exceptional cases mention *theos* explicitly
when dealing with Christ's resurrection and never directly talk about the God of
Israel, the fathers etc. in this connection.

[8]   Of fourteen occurences of *anistēmi* used transitively in the New Testament, Luke
alone has ten in various contexts, the rest are in John 6:39ff.

[9]   The only exceptions are 6:8 and 8:6: Stephen and Philip actively performed
miracles, however, because they are filled with divine miracle power, *dynamis*, 6:8.

when it is said that the risen Jesus performs miracles, it is God who does them through the name of Jesus (3:6,16; 4:30).[10] What is decisive for Luke is not that miracles happen, but that they are miracles of the God of Israel. The wonders are always connected to the preaching and serve to show the irresistible nature of the word of God.[11] Proclamation and miracle belong in essence together.

A serious problem for the Jewish Christians is mission among non-Jews. Salvation, according to the Jews, is reserved for Israel, the people of the law of God. How is it possible to offer salvation to non-Jews, Gentiles, who are, by definition, the enemies of Israel, and who have not accepted the law of God? Luke tries to mitigate the problem through the notion that the Gentiles wanted by the church are the God-fearers, who are accepted by the synagogue.[12] A further argument for the legitimacy of the mission among the Gentiles is to demonstrate it to be a part of the promises given to Israel.[13] But the main argument is that the God of Israel himself has forced the church to accept Gentiles as members of the church, even if God is never given a title like 'the God of the nations'. This irresistible force of God for accepting Gentiles is shown in the story of Cornelius (10–11; 15:7–10,14); God forces Peter under protest to proclaim the gospel to Cornelius and then to baptize him. The whole Gentile mission occurs for the sake of the name of God (15:14); God's approval of the Gentile mission is shown by his bestowing upon them the Holy Spirit (10:44f.; 11:17; 15:8); their lack of the law is recovered, as God has purified their hearts (15:9), and even in the daily work of the mission God is always the acting force (14:3,27; 15:4,12; 18:21; 21:19; 22:14; 26:22). The missionary work is, according to the Scriptures, seen as God's

---

[10]   Only in 9:34 do we find the active form, 'Jesus Christ heals you.' But where Luke renders traditional miracle stories (3:1–10; 9:32ff.,36–43; 13:10ff.; 14:11ff.; 16:18ff.; 20:7–12; 28:8ff.) he does not rework or rewrite them, but interprets them with help of his wonder-summaries.

[11]   J. Jervell, *Unknown Paul*, 85ff. The miracle material is insubstantial in relation to the speech material.

[12]   Luke is the only author within the New Testament for whom the God-fearers play a role.

[13]   Cf. the section below, 'Crisis: the divided people of God'.

rebuilding of 'the fallen house of David', Israel, and its outcome is that the Gentiles may seek the Lord (15:16–18).

The church regards itself as the people of God, not *a* people, but *the* only people. And there is but one people of God, namely Israel. The church is Israel. It is therefore necessary for Luke to show that God has a people, that this people has a unique history with God and that this people still exists as God's people.

God has one people of his own. Luke has no interest in any other people; that is shown in his terminology, as he uses *laos*, a word reserved for Israel. The word is used in the New Testament 142 times; by Luke alone 84 times, that is 60 per cent of the total. When he uses the word in an unqualified way, he always has in mind Israel as a nation. Sometimes it means 'crowd', a synonym for *ochlos*, but signifying a crowd of Jews.[14] Israel is not a nation among other nations, but always *the* people.[15] When it comes to other peoples, Luke employs from the Septuagint the plural – 'all the peoples'[16] – that is the peoples, nations, in their totality as opposed to Israel.[17] Only Israel is a people from a biblical viewpoint. When Luke makes a list of peoples (Acts 2:9ff.), it concerns not the peoples as such, but the Dispersion, the Jews living among other nations outside Palestine (2:5,11). The world outside Israel is the Dispersion (Acts 1:8; 2:5). Luke's idea of the mission is not to 'make all nations my disciples' (Matt. 28:19), but to proclaim the gospel 'to the ends of the earth' (Acts 1:8), which means a mission in the Dispersion, clearly seen from Acts 13–28. Only Luke in the New Testament

---

[14] There are two exceptions: Acts 15:14, 'a people from the Gentiles'; that is, Luke cannot name the Gentiles in the church 'people', but has to qualify them as a crowd from the Gentiles. See also Acts 18:10.

[15] *Laos* is used once in the plural of Israel (4:25,27), but then as a quotation from the Scriptures.

[16] The singular is found in Acts 7:7, but as a scriptural quotation.

[17] Luke never talks about 'the Roman people', but always about 'the Romans' (Acts 2:10; 16:21,37,38; 22:25,26,27,29; 23:27; 25:16). Luke is interested in Rome as a political and geographical entity, but not in a people of Rome. 'The Greeks' does not signify a nation, but non-Jews, Gentiles from various nationalities around Israel, in Acts 9:29; 11:20 14:1; 18:4; 19:10,17; 20:21.

addresses Jews as Israelites (Acts 2:22; 3:12; 5:35; 13:16; 21:28).[18]

What constitutes Israel as the only people of God is God's election of this people, starting with God choosing Abraham and the fathers (Acts 7:1ff.; 13:17ff.). Israel is from the beginning of its history signified as church, and the only people in the world with the right to be church. Why God has chosen this people Luke never explains. Israel's unique position among the nations is demonstrated by the fact that only Israel has a history, that is a history where God has acted and still acts. In the New Testament the history of Israel is either presupposed or mentioned in a fragmentary manner.[19] But Luke has two detailed accounts of this history in continuous résumés (Acts 7:2–53; 13:16–25), and further repeated allusions to particular events of this history. The surveys in Acts 7 and 13 serve as the premise for the church as they show the first and constitutional phase of the history of the church. This is necessary because the church of Luke has severe problems with its identity. If it were not itself a part of the history of the people of God, there would be no people of God and no church. Consequently the history of Israel has never come to an end, but continues in linear progression into the church. The God well known to Israel is wholly unknown to the Gentiles, and so their history is a story of ignorance and idolatry. The church is not a part of their history, not even for the Gentiles in the church, but stems solely from the story of the people of God. Only Israel has Abraham as its father and only in the history of Israel do you find the 'fathers', for whom God acted throughout history (Acts 3:13,25; 4:25; 5:30; 7:11,12,15,19,32,38,39,44,51,52; 13:17,32,36; 15:10; 22:14; 26:6; 28:25). The promises of salvation are given solely to Israel (Luke 2:29; Acts 2:39; 3:25; 13:47; 28:25). There is but one people of salvation, and the people is saved as a people. Salvation is at its peak in the resurrection of the dead, which is called 'the hope of Israel' (Acts 23:6; 26:6; 28:20). Resurrection is the aim of the worship of Israel (Acts 26:7).

The pre-Christian history of the chosen people is marked by

---

[18] Once 'Jews', 2:14.
[19] E.g. Rom. 4:1ff.; 11:1ff.; Gal. 3:16ff.; 4:24ff.; Hebr. 11:1ff.

faithlessness and corruption. On the one hand stand God's promises, guidance and benefits, on the other the sins of the people. God's answer to the faithlessness of his people is constant new promises. He fulfils his promises to his corrupt people. The backbone of God's acts is not the faithfulness or faithlessness, sins or piety of the people, but only his faithfulness, patience and grace (Acts 13:17–25). In spite of the sins of the people God has never rejected Israel; it is forever the chosen people of God destined for salvation. Israel is corrupt, it is the fallen house of David (Acts 15:16ff.), but it is not rejected. If God actually had rejected Israel, there could be no church.

The final epoch in the history of Israel is the epoch of the church; Israel at the end of times is a people in crisis. The final saving act in the history Luke introduces in a characteristic way: 'Will you establish once again the kingdom to Israel?' (Acts 1:6).[20] And God will return and rebuild the fallen house of David from its ruins and set it up again (Acts 15:16).[21] The story continues with the Messiah-Jesus.

THE MESSIAH FOR THE PEOPLE

Has the church any right to confess its faith in Jesus the Messiah? Is the resurrected Jesus the promised Messiah of Israel? Luke provides his church with an answer. He knows that salvation is given only to the people of God and comes from no one but the Messiah, who stems from that same people. Everything in the church hangs on belief in the true Messiah. Luke knows that his church has doubts and a great need for 'assurance concerning the instruction' they have received (Luke 1:4). The members of the church mostly came from a synagogue denying any right to proclaim Jesus as the promised Messiah; as

---

[20] Repeatedly this saying has been understood as a relapse into Jewish nationalism, which is being corrected by Jesus. But there is not the slightest hint of any correction. The salvation seen as the re-establishment of Israel: Luke 1:32; 24:21; Acts 2:30ff.; 15:16ff.

[21] The 'restoration of the fallen house of David' has to do with Israel as the people of God. As this seem unlikely in the mouth of a supposed Gentile Christian like Luke, it has been suggested that v. 16 expresses 'the story of Jesus culminating in the resurrection', so E. Haenchen, *The Acts of the Apostles*, Oxford 1971, 448. Nothing justifies such an interpretation.

the church also had Gentile members, coming from Israel's adversaries, and even a Jewish apostate, Paul, as the first missionary, there were reasons for doubt. Did Jesus actually have messianic status? Here we have the setting for Luke's dealing with christology, which exegetes have found peculiar if intended for Gentile Christians.[22]

The christology of Acts is designed for Christians of a Jewish origin. The distinctive christology of Luke can be identified as what we might safely call Jewish-Christian, closely related to the Scriptures and Jewish traditions. This christology cannot be labelled 'historic' in the sense that it held up to Luke's readers and church the christology of their Christian forefathers in the church in Jerusalem, as though it had no bearing on the thinking and credo of Luke's own church.[23]

In the Gospel of Luke christology is worked out above all by a series of stories, rarely by titles and never by exact definitions of the identity of Jesus. When writing Acts Luke obviously assumed that his readers knew those stories. For obvious reasons we do not find the stories from the life of Jesus in Acts, and here Luke prefers to form his christology by the use of titles. He has a highly independent and distinctive selection and use of titles.[24] He employs some seemingly very old christological titles, mostly only to be found in Luke's works within the New Testament, and going back to the church in Jerusalem: Jesus is 'the holy' (2:27 (OT quotation); 3:14); 'the righteous one' (3:14; 7:52);[25] God's true agent to Israel (22:14);[26] *pais*,[27] God's servant[28] (3:13,26; 4:25,27,30); his portrayal as one of the men of God in the Scriptures (Luke 1:54) and as 'the prophet' (Acts

---

[22]   Cf. H. Conzelmann, *Die Mitte der Zeit*, BHTh 17, Tübingen 1954, 158ff.

[23]   The clear primitive, pre-Pauline character of Luke's christology has nothing to do with Luke acting as a historian. This christology, different from a Hellenistic, Gentile-Christian christology, is the only suitable one for Luke's church.

[24]   For a survey of the literature on christological titles see F. Bovon, *Luke the Theologian: Thirty-Three Years of Research*, Allison Park, PA, 1987, 177–97.

[25]   Cf. Rev. 16:5.

[26]   Cf. Luke 1:17; 23:50; Acts 10:22.

[27]   The term is a title not only for Jesus but for David and Israel, Luke 1:54.

[28]   The translation 'child' is impossible as Luke even characterizes David and Israel as *pais*, Luke 1:54,69; Acts 4:24. In Luke 2:43 it means 'child', Jesus as child, but here we have a different form from the ones in Acts where *pais* always is related to God: *pais sou, pais autou*.

3:22f.; 7:37)[29] puts Jesus in line with the prophets of the Scriptures (Luke 9:8,19), representing 'the climax of God's continuing saving activity through them';[30] above all, Jesus is the prophet like Moses, the eschatological prophet (Acts 7:37), who even restores the original Mosaic Torah; Jesus is leader, prince (Acts 3:15; 5:31)[31] – Jesus is the fulfilment of the Davidic hope.

The most significant title is *Christos*, stemming from Palestinian Judaism and determining the other, different titles.[32] When Luke was writing Acts, the original title *Christos* had long since become a proper name in christological development, but Luke uses it again as a title.[33] The title is not used primarily to show the relation between God and Jesus, but is attached to the scheme of promise–fulfilment: Jesus fulfils the promises to the people of God. Jesus is the anointed of Israel, and this applies as well to the earthly as to the risen Jesus. The title is not merely tradition; Luke uses it etymologically and gives it a definition unintelligible to non-Jews (Luke 4:18; Acts 4:27; 10:38).[34] The Messiah is thoroughly the Old Testament figure (Luke 2:26; 3:15; 24:19–46; Acts 2:31); Jesus is 'the Lord's [i.e. God's] Messiah' (Luke 2:26; 9:20; 23:35; Acts 4:26); Luke can also use it for the Old Testament Messiah without any special reference to Jesus (Luke 2:26; 3:15; 24:24–6). Messiah-Jesus is God's agent as the bearer of salvation to Israel. Peculiar to Luke is that this Messiah of Israel is a suffering Messiah (Acts 3:18; 17:3; 26:23; Luke 24:26,46). This idea is unknown to the Old Testament and to Jewish literature prior to or contemporaneous with the New Testament. Luke accompanies each reference to the suffering Messiah with the strongly emphasized and detailed

---

[29] Cf. Luke 7:16; 9:8,19; 13:33; 24:19.

[30] E. Franklin, *Christ the Lord. A Study in the Purpose and Theology of Luke–Acts*, London 1975, 67.

[31] Apart from Acts only Hebr. 2:10; 12:2.

[32] In the christological title employed by Luke there is no distinction between the earthly and the exalted Christ as if we had to do with two different epochs theologically.

[33] Thus even if Luke can use *Christos* as a sort of a second name in 'Jesus Christ', this is dependent upon his use of the term as a title. Luke knows what happened to the title.

[34] The title as such was unintelligible to Greeks.

assertion that this is exactly what the Scriptures say: Moses, all the prophets, the psalms. The idea is that the God of Israel foretold and foreordained this suffering, expressed through the divine *dei* ('it is necessary'), or through direct reference to God (Acts 3:18; 17:3; Luke 24:26). When Israel does not know and acknowledge its suffering Messiah, the explanation is the ignorance of the people (Acts 3:17); even the disciples did not understand his sufferings, because they did not understand and believe the Scriptures (Luke 24:26,45f.). The suffering Messiah is not an invention of the church, but the testimony of old from God himself.

A variant of *Christos* is 'the Son of David': this title is used by Luke more than by any other New Testament writer. The title is, to Luke, not merely tradition. Luke knows the title 'the Son of David' (Luke 18:38f.; 20:41), but does not employ it at all in Acts, even though he repeatedly deals with the matter involved in the title. Luke's language is different from that of the rest of the New Testament.[35] He uses the title in the most independent way, not primarily from his Christian tradition, but viewed against the background of the Old Testament and the Jewish tradition.[36] As the Son of David, Jesus fulfils the promises to David about restoring David's kingdom for Israel (Luke 1:32f.,69; 2:26; 3:15; 24:24-46; Acts 2:29-36; 13:32,34-7; 15:15-18). Now Jesus is 'the king', the king of the Jews (Luke 19:38; 23:2,3,37,38; Acts 17:7);[37] the title carries for Luke a political connotation (Luke 23:2; Acts 17:7). The Messiah-king is the one Israel expected to come. Luke uses christological titles familiar to Jews, but avoids what may be intelligible to non-Jews. The title 'Son of God' appears only once in Acts (9:20).[38]

---

35 Examples: Luke 1:16,32,54,67,69; 2:4; Acts 2:29; 4:25; 7:46; 13:34; 15:16.
36 Cf. C. Burger, *Jesus als Davidssohn. Eine traditionsgeschichtliche Untersuchung*, FRLANT 98, Göttingen 1979, 137-52. The Old Testament dominance over Luke's christology is so clear 'that he does not always give full expression to the experience of the early Christian community': E. Franklin, *Christ the Lord*, 55. A study of later manuscripts shows their dissatisfaction that Luke used the title in accordance with Jewish thought.
37 Luke is the only evangelist who introduces Jesus as king into the quotation from Ps. 118:26: Luke 19:38.
38 We find the title in some late manuscripts in Acts 8:37, and five times in Luke's Gospel. The title is said to demonstrate the unique relationship between Jesus and

When 'Saviour' is mentioned, it refers to the saviour of Israel and descendant of David (Luke 1:47 used of God; 2:11; Acts 5:31; 13:23); the background is the Old Testament.[39] The resurrected Jesus is the Son of David. There is no Messiah without the people, i.e. Israel. Jesus is 'the climax of God's activity in Israel'.[40]

Numerically, Luke's favourite title is *kyrios*, 'Lord', used of both God[41] and Jesus. The earthly Jesus is called as *kyrios*, and it also applies to him after the resurrection. In using the title of both God and Jesus, Luke in some sense regarded Jesus as on a level with God. This is the only epithet of God transferred to Jesus, and the subordinate character of the christology is preserved. The title is expressive of the dominion that both have over Israel: as Lord and Davidic king Jesus re-establishes the people of God (Luke 1:32,35; 2:11; 20:44; Acts 1:6; 2:25ff.,36).[42] Often *Christos* and *kyrios* are combined and used interchangeably (Luke 2:11,26; 24:3; Acts 2:36; 4:26; 11:17; 15:26). As *kyrios* Jesus is the kingly Messiah.

Luke also presents Jesus as a Palestinian Jew. Jesus is the Son of the people, of Israel. Nothing like a title 'Son of Israel' exists for Luke, but the idea is present. The simple fact that Jesus was a Jew, a fact that no author in the New Testament denies or discusses, Luke elaborates in a most independent way, giving it christological rank. What is important is not that Jesus was a man, but that he was a Jewish man. He did not come down from heaven, but was a Jew born in Bethlehem of Davidic lineage (Luke 1:27; 2:4; 3:31). In the Gospel of Luke, this emphasis is found in the material peculiar to Luke: the circumcision of Jesus, as one of

---

God, but shows the divine, miraculous power Jesus had. It is remarkable that there is no hint whatsoever in Acts of this title related to the virginal conception through the Holy Spirit, Luke 1:34–5.

[39] Usually this title is mentioned as useful for Hellenistic readers, but what about the Jewish content Luke provides?

[40] E. Franklin, *Christ the Lord*, 7.

[41] In pre-Christian Palestine Jews spoke of God as *'dwn*, 'Lord', (Aramaic: *mara*, Greek: *kurios*).

[42] Acts 10:36, where Jesus is named 'Lord of all', is not opposed to this, for in the speech 10:34–43 the subject is Jesus' ministry in Israel, and the God-fearer, Cornelius, is incorporated in Israel.

the people (2:21); the presentation as a first-born in the temple (2:22–4); Jesus as a boy and very gifted pupil in the temple (2:41–52); the genealogy, which shows him to be a descendant of David, in a succession of many sons of David, and of the people (3:23–38).[43] He is throughout the Gospel depicted with notably human, that is Jewish, qualities. In Acts the emphasis is present in the two historical surveys (7:2–53, esp. v. 37, and 13:17–25, esp. v. 23). Here Jesus falls into line with the history of the people. He is incorporated in Israel itself.

The accumulation of christological titles is characteristic. This has nothing to do with a dependence on tradition, as if Luke were trying to collect all christological titles; some of the titles known from the church are missing, and Luke employs the titles in a most independent way, going back above all to the Scriptures. It has to do with Luke's stressing the 'all'; he is talking about all the prophets, all God's word, all Jesus has said and done etc. And so there is no messianic title, epithet or name from the Scriptures which does not apply to Jesus. The multiplicity testifies to Luke's biblicism, his appeal to the Scriptures of Israel. This even explains the absence of some titles which reveal forms of metaphysical speculation in christology. Jesus is not divine, not pre-existent, not incarnated, not the creator or tool of creation, not the universal reconciler, not the *imago dei* etc.

In Jesus Christ, God's activity in the history of Israel is manifested. The key figure in this history, and so also in christology, is God himself. God is the saviour, even when salvation is tied to the Christ-event (Acts 4:12). God himself is the very centre of christology, something demonstrated by Luke's heavy employment of the Scriptures, which he understands as the revelation of God's will, works and words throughout history, including the Christ-event. Within the New Testament, only Luke describes the main events in christology, the suffering, death and resurrection of Jesus, by proofs from

---

[43]   The genealogies in Judaism served to show that a person belonged not to a certain family, but to the people: cf. J. Jeremias, *Jerusalem in the Time of Jesus*, London [4] 1979, 275ff.; M.D. Johnson, *The Purpose of the Biblical Genealogies with Special Reference to the Setting of the Genealogies of Jesus*, SNTSMS 8, Cambridge 1969, 97.

the Scriptures (Acts 2:24ff.,30ff.; 3:18ff.; 4:10ff.; 13:33ff.; 17:2ff.; 26:22f.; Luke18:31ff.; 24:26ff.,44ff.). Even when Luke refers to Jesus' prediction of his passion and resurrection found in the tradition, he adds to the third prediction: 'everything that is written ... by the prophets must be accomplished' (Luke 18:31). He means by this that Jesus' death is according to God's will; the death and the resurrection are solely God's work. Luke gets Jesus' prediction about his passion and resurrection from the tradition, but it is important to him that he links it with the Scriptures. It follows that the suffering and death of Christ are not explicitly defined as sacrifice and atonement, and we have no theory about expiation.[44] But, more importantly, the death is first and foremost a part of the Scriptures, a fulfilment, the death predetermined by God as the result of Christ's obedience and of the sins of the Jews. Luke does not only present proofs from the Scriptures that Christ was raised from the dead, but he even has to give 'negative' scriptural proof. It was not David but his son whom God raised from the dead, whereas David remained in his grave (Acts 2:29ff.; 13:36).

The climax of God's acts in Christ is the resurrection, and everything hangs on this as the act of Israel's God. Luke alone in the New Testament speaks of 'proofs' of the resurrection, which probably shows that doubts had emerged in Christian circles (cf. Luke 24:11,21,38). What happened in the forty days after the resurrection was to show, above all, the reality, not simply of the resurrection as such, but of the resurrection of Jesus: the disciples did not see a ghost (Luke 24:37); he ate broiled fish with the disciples on Easter Sunday (Luke 24:43; Acts 10:41), and he experienced no decay (Acts 2:27; 13:35–7). Apart from this proof from the Scriptures Luke gives his account in a language peculiar to him: he uses the transitive verbs *anastēsai* and *egeirein*; the latter verb he uses in the active with God as the subject (Acts 3:15; 4:10; 5:30; 10:41; 17:3, cf. 26:8); this is to be found only in Acts within the New Testament. It is necessary for Luke explicitly to mention God when using the verb *egeirein* of Jesus' resurrection. He uses the passive,

---

[44] But Luke knew about Jesus' death having saving significance, as atonement: Luke 22:19b–20; Acts 20:28.

ēgerthē, only twice, in Luke 9:22; 24:34, but this is obviously from
the tradition;[45] in the passive God is the implied agent.[46] The
transitive, *anastēsai*, 'raise', is used in the active, God as subject
for the resurrection (Acts 2:22,32; 3:26; 13:33,34; 17:31). The
intransitive, *anastēnai*, 'rise' (Luke 18:33; 24:7,46; Acts 10:41;
17:3), is the traditional way of referring to the resurrection.
Luke obviously knows this and refers to it, however seldom, but
prefers to employ a different vocabulary. The difference is that
Luke's form ascribes the cause of Christ's resurrection to God,
whereas the other implies that Jesus rose by his own power.[47]
The oldest form of the kerygma stresses God as causative: God
is the one who raises the dead (Acts 26:8), God has intervened –
and Luke has returned to that form. For him everything hangs
upon the God of Israel having raised Jesus: 'The God of our
fathers raised up Jesus' (Acts 5:30).

The difference in vocabulary shows that the Lucan christology has a tone of subordination: God is at its centre and
Jesus is managed by his Father. The whole salvation is God's,
and so Luke writes: 'Jesus of Nazareth, a man singled out by
God and made known to you through miracles, portents and
signs, which God worked among you through him' (Acts 2:22).
Christ is the tool of salvation. In different ways Luke underlines
Christ's subordination. It is already found in the reference to
the Scriptures: God speaks in the Scriptures, whereas Christ is
spoken of. Titles and epithets connected with God are not
transferred to Christ, as we find in other parts of the New
Testament; only God is *theos*, *despotēs* (Acts 4:24; Luke 2:29),
Father, creator (Acts 4:24; 14:15; 17:24), and Christ is not even
seen as a tool. Some functions are reserved for God: the angels
are not subordinate to Christ, only to God (Acts 5:19; 8:26; 12:7;
Luke 4:10; 22:43); Christ prays to his Father; the Spirit belongs
to God and is given solely by God, even to Christ, who transfers

---

[45]   Mark 14:28; 16:6; Matt. 17:9,23; 20:19; 26:32; 28:6.

[46]   The passive can only be translated 'was raised' (by God) and not, intransitively,
'rise', cf. J.A. Fitzmyer, *The Gospel According to Luke* I, Anch.B, New York 1981, 195f.

[47]   1 Thess. 4:14; Mark 8:31; 9:9,31; 10:34; 16:6; John 20:9. The furthest from Luke and
the old kerygma is found in John: cf. John 10:17, Jesus has the power to take his life
again; the sayings about Jesus raising people from the dead, and John 12:1,9,17,
Jesus raising the dead.

the gift given to him to men (Acts 1:4,8; 2:33; 5:32; Luke 24:49). The work of salvation is God's work, as is set out in Acts 1:7, and Christ the tool; all Christ's honours are bestowed upon him by God (Acts 2:36).

We find the same in the ascension. Luke is the writer in the New Testament, *par exellence*, who refers to Christ as ascended and exalted (Acts 1:2,9,11; 2:33; 5:31; 7:56; Luke 9:51; 22:69; 24:51). Luke's vocabulary is characteristic: he uses the words *analambanein* in the passive (Acts 1:2,11,22), *anapherein* in the passive (Luke 24:51) and *epairō* in the passive (Acts 1:9), 'was taken up, carried up', the implied subject is God, or *hypsoō* in the passive (Acts 2:33), 'was exalted', (active, 5:31: 'God exalted him'). There can be no doubt in the church: God himself, the God of Israel, has intervened and has given Christ his proper status. The exaltation is therefore seen as enthronement; Jesus has received the promises to David and is placed on the throne of David (Acts 2:29–36; 13:33ff.). And he is appointed as a Messiah still to come (Acts 3:20–1).

In Acts, the exalted Christ is a remarkably passive figure and it is hard to see that he has any real function. Acts 1:11 goes directly from his ascension to his return. His function is limited to the ideas that he is at the right hand of the Father, has poured out the Spirit and will be involved in the judgement of the world (Acts 2:33f.; 5:31; 7:55f.; 10:42; 17:31; Luke 22:69). Jesus is received in heaven until the times of restitution (Acts 3:21). The saying that Jesus intercedes for us[48] is not to be found in Acts. It is important to Luke to demonstrate that the God of Israel is the active power in and behind the church – hence the passivity of the exalted Christ. Christ's role is expressed through the use of 'the name'.[49] The idea is not that the exalted Christ as person is present in the church or in the missionary work, for he resides in heaven until the parousia, but that the life, death and resurrection of Christ show the way God acts. Therefore the name never occurs as subject of the various sayings and acts which takes place in connection with it. Other

[48] Rom. 8:34; Heb. 7:25; 9:24.
[49] Of 238 occurrences of *onoma* in the New Testament, Luke alone has 94, and 60 in Acts.

people act in or by the name: the apostles and missionaries speak and teach in his name (Acts 4:17,18; 8:12; 9:15,27f.), perform miracles in his name (3:6; 4:7,10,30),[50] suffer for the name (9:16; 15:26; 21:13), receive forgiveness and salvation through his name (10:43), are being baptized in the name (2:38; 10:48; 19:5). When they invoke the name, God himself takes action (2:21; 4:30; 22:16). And when the church 'from among the Gentiles' in association with the restored Israel is labelled 'a people for his name', it has to do with the name of God (15:14,17).

The driving force of Luke's christology is not some notion of a constitutive salvation-history with Jesus as the decisive 'mid-point of time'.[51] But the christological frame is the history of the people of God, or God's history with his people. And so the christology has to be seen as the climax of God's activity in Israel and, through Israel, with 'the rest of mankind' (Acts 15:14ff.). Was the Christ-event actually a part of the history of the people of God? The answer to this determines Luke's idea of Christ.

CRISIS: THE DIVIDED PEOPLE OF GOD

What Luke has to say about the church, and so the pressing question of the identity of the Christians, we may summarize thus: the church is Israel in the final act of its history. Luke does not speak of the Christians primarily as 'church', but as a people, *laos*, the word reserved for Israel in its unique position. Israel plays an important role in Luke's theology: 'Israel' and 'the people' are, apart from two exceptions,[52] always mentioned in one sense – Israel as the people of God – and

---

[50]   Only once in Acts do we find a miracle performed directly from the exalted Christ (9:34), but the meaning is exactly the same as in 2:22; 4:30: God performs all the miracles of Christ. Cf. further Acts 3:16, where Luke rewrites a tradition with the simple saying that the name works a miracle into the utterance that the faith in the name was decisive.

[51]   The delay of the parousia is no problem to Luke. Therefore, there is no constitutive salvation-history with various epochs and with Jesus as 'the midpoint of time' as a substitute for the imminent return of Christ. *Contra* the very influential work of H. Conzelmann, *The Theology of St Luke*, London 1960.

[52]   Acts 15:14; 18:6.

there is but one people of God, there can never be another. The church is a part of that people and represents that people. Of 192 occurrences of 'the Jews' in the New Testament, Luke alone has 84,[53] mostly in a positive sense. The forefathers of the Christians are 'the fathers', that is the former Israelites, not the first generations of Christians. 'The fathers' are mentioned a few times (ten) elsewhere in the New Testament, and do not play any significant role; to Luke they are an important subject of his reflections, mentioned in Acts alone more than thirty times.

When the Messiah arrives the people of God is a people in crisis. Messiah reinforces the crisis and brings it to a climax, dividing the people into two parts. The task and programme of the Messiah are clear: he is going to restore the kingdom to Israel (Acts 1:6; 15:14ff.). The house of David is fallen and in ruins, and the Messiah is going to rebuild it (Acts 1:6); there is no king on the throne of David (Luke 1:32f.; Acts 2:30); the decay of the people, and so its crisis, come from its sins. This we find in the résumé of the history of Israel (Acts 7:2–53). Remarkably enough, the sins are not of a moral kind, but have always to do with an opposition to God's acts in the history of the people (7:9,25ff.,35,38ff.,49ff.,52f.). The climax of the people's sins is the murder of the Messiah (2:23; 3:15; 4:10; 5:30; 7:52; 10:39; 13:28).

The outcome of this history should have been that God had rejected his people, that the history of Israel had come to an end, and that Israel itself had become a thing of the past. If this had been the case, for Luke there would have been no church. For all the promises of salvation belong as ever to the people, and they are hereditary (Acts 2:39; 3:25ff.; 10:40ff.; 13:26ff.). God's answer to the faithlessness of his people has been to renew his promises (7:5–8,10,16,17ff.,33f.,35–8). In spite of the people's idolatry and the persecution of the prophets, God has sent his Messiah. What is decisive is neither the faithlessness nor the faithfulness of the people, but rather the faithfulness and grace of God (Acts 13:17–25).

---

[53] The rest we find in John, and there to a great extent in a negative sense.

The fate of Israel, in particular the effect the coming of the Messiah had on Israel, is a burning question for Luke. The whole of the early church worked hard on this question, not because of some interest in history as such, but because the fate of Israel was the clue to the problem of the identity of the church. And the answers differ in various churches.[54]

What about Luke? For years interpreters found a solution in the salvation-history in Luke–Acts: Israel was past history. The Jewish people had rejected the Christian proclamation and, for that reason, had themselves been rejected. The church of the Gentiles continued the history of the old people, but was not seen as Israel, but rather as a new kind of people, a church. Luke is seen as indifferent to the faith of Israel.

In fact, Luke sees the situation quite differently: Israel has become the divided people of God. Striking remarks in Acts relate the great success of the Christian mission to the Jews. Mass conversions of Jews are again and again reported;[55] these reports are concerned with the conversion of Jews, and Luke is less concerned to narrate the conversion of Gentiles. Instances of the latter also occur, though less often, and have to do mainly with conversions among 'God-fearing' Gentiles, who are already related to Israel via the synagogue (Acts 13:43; 14:1; 17:4,12); the 'prototype' for the Gentile convert is the 'God-fearing' Cornelius (10:1ff.). Mass conversions have primarily taken place in Jerusalem, owing to the significance of Jerusalem for Israel and so for the church. The result is that tens of thousands of pious Jews have become believers (21:20). Thus a large part of Israel accepts the gospel. Significantly, those Jews who are faithful to the law, the most Jewish Jews, become believers (2:41; 6:7; 17:11ff.; 21:20). And all the God-fearers are, by definition, pious people.

Israel is becoming a divided people over the issue of the Messiah. This is the crisis. Hand in hand with the reports of conversions are accounts of the opposition that the missionaries encounter, principally from Jews. There is a striking

---

54   See chapter four, 'Acts and the New Testament'.
55   There have been numerous attempts to play down the importance of the reports of mass conversion.

juxtaposition of Jewish conversion and opposition, whereas the attitude of Gentiles interests Luke less, as, in contrast to the rejection of the gospel on the part of the Jews, it does not have a special theological interest. The interplay between rejection and acceptance of the gospel is clear throughout Acts as a whole: the consequences of Peter's speech at the temple (3:11–26) are persecution of the missionaries (4:1ff.) and mass conversion (4:4). Before the second trial (5:17ff.) there comes an overwhelming growth in the church (5:14).[56] Before the execution of Stephen and the resulting persecution we have reports of the success of the mission, especially among the Jerusalem priests (6:7). After the Jerusalem scenes comes the Dispersion, where the preaching takes place in the synagogues. The outcome is the same: the appearance of the missionaries in Pisidian Antioch results first in Jewish conversions and then in opposition (13:42f.,45); Jews and others become believers in Iconium, while the unrepentant Jews incite persecution (14:2ff.); some Jews are converted in Thessalonica, while others begin a new persecution (17:5f.); the Jews in Beroea receive the missionaries with open minds and we have a mass conversion among them, but then we have an incitement of the population by Jews from Thessalonica (17:12). The pattern is always the same: conversion and opposition, which turns into persecution. The Jewish people did not reject the gospel *en bloc* – not even an overwhelming majority of Jews oppose the message – rather, from the beginning the mission to Jews was very successful, so that a significant portion of the people was converted, 'tens of thousands who were zealous for the law' (21:20). The success among the Jews continued after the way to the Gentiles was opened (Acts 10–11).

Israel has not rejected the gospel, but has become divided over the issue. The church is a church primarily of Jews and for the Jews. The identity of the church, then, is clear: it is Israel, the one and only. The Christians are heirs of the promises to Israel, and they are so as Jews. This is expressed in a variety of

---

[56] Notice the awkward place of the verse in the context, breaking up the clear connection between vv. 13 and 14. The intention is that despite the caution of some Jews great crowds have been converted.

ways. Luke emphasizes that the earliest Jerusalem Christians lived as pious Jews: they frequent the temple, live in strictest observance of the law and in accordance with the customs of the fathers, precisely because they hope for the restoration of Israel (2:46; 3:1; 5:12; 10:9ff.; 11:2; 15:1ff.; 16:3; 21:20). All accusations that the Christians did not live according to the law, or even opposed the law, are repudiated (6:11,13f.; 10:14,28; 21:21,28; 28:17). Paul was and is a Pharisee and a Jew who is faithful to the law (22:3; 23:1,3,5,6; 24:14; 26:4–5).[57] The church believes and teaches everything that is written in the law and the prophets (24:14f.; 26:22f.). Paul is charged because he preaches the resurrection, but the resurrection expresses God's promises to his people and the hope of pharisaic Israel (23:6; 24:21; 26:26–8). Belief in the resurrection means fidelity to Scripture, law and people (24:14ff.; 26:22f.). Above all, the preaching of the church takes place in the synagogues, as these are 'churches' even to Christians (13:14ff.; 14:1ff.; 16:13ff.; 17:1ff.,10ff.,17; 18:4ff.,26).[58] The Jews in the Dispersion who have been won for the gospel do not emerge as an independent group (19:8ff.; 26:11). Luke's use of the address *andres adelphoi* (Acts 1:16; 2:29,37; 13:15,26,38; 15:13; 22:1; 23:1; 28:17) shows a consciousness of being Israel; this address is not restricted to the Christian community. Even if Luke does call Christians 'brothers', this is not his most typical usage, for he uses this form throughout Acts as a Jewish address and consistently avoids it for Gentiles (2:29,37; 3:17; 7:2,23,25; 13:26,38; 22:1; 23:1,6; 28:17). There must be a considerable number of Jews in the church in order to substantiate the claim to be Israel and represent Israel. That is what the accounts of mass conversions mean for Luke. What about the unbelieving section among the people? Luke calls them 'Jews' throughout Acts,[59] but they do

---

57 This adherence to the law and the Jewishness of Acts is mostly explained as history: for Luke, it belongs to the past, as Luke himself testifies to a Hellenistic Christianity where there is no strict adherence to the law (cf. F. Bovon, *Das Evangelium des Lukas* [Luke 1:1 – 9:50], EKK III/1, Neukirchen 1989, 25). This understanding is, however, in conflict with Luke's understanding of history as salvation-history which places obligations on the present: J. Jervell, *Retrospect and Prospect in Luke–Acts Interpretation*, SBL Seminar Papers 1991, 387ff.

58 Cf. J. Jervell, *Unknown Paul*, 135.

59 Cf. Rev. 2:9: some claim to be Jews, but are not.

not any more represent Israel (3:11–26). By use of a quotation from Deuteronomy 18 Luke speaks of Jesus as a prophet whose mission to Israel Moses had prophesied (3:22f.): this means that anyone who has not heeded the prophet's words should be rooted out from the people. The rejection of the preaching results in the purging of the unrepentant portion of the people, being 'extirpated from Israel' (3:23).

The claim to be and to represent Israel depends on the members of the church being themselves Jews; according to the accounts of mass conversions they certainly are. On the other hand there are Gentiles, non-Jews, in the church. How can this be reconciled with the claim? The Gentiles of the church are God-fearers,[60] Gentiles who were admitted into and accepted by the synagogue, even if they were not full members of the people. They were, so to say, the God-fearers in the church which consisted of Jews. But they had the same rights as the Jews in the church, and if they were present in considerable numbers, perhaps a majority, how could the church still claim to be Israel? Luke has to explain and defend the mission among Gentiles and their position within the church. What is the relation between the people of God and the nations? Even sixty years after the death of Christ the mission among the Gentiles poses a problem.

Through the interpretation of the resurrection of Jesus and the mass conversions Luke sketches a picture of Israel for whom the promises are fulfilled, for the enthronement of the Messiah on David's throne has taken place (Acts 2:29–36) and a great part of the people has been converted. The story of the acceptance of the Gentiles starts with Cornelius in Acts 10–11. This story is explained in James' speech at the Apostolic Council in 15:13–21:

After this I will return, and I will rebuild the dwelling of David, which has fallen; I will rebuild its ruins, and I will set it up, that the rest of men may seek the Lord, and all the Gentiles who are called by my name, says the Lord, who made these things known from of old.[61]

---

[60] J. Jervell, 'The Church of Jews and God-fearers', in J.B. Tyson (ed.), *Luke–Acts and the Jewish People. Eight Critical Perspectives*, Minneapolis 1988, 11–20.

[61] LXX Amos 9:11, influenced by Jer. 12:15.

The Scriptures say that God will first rebuild and restore Israel, and then, as a result of this event, the Gentiles will seek the Lord. The Cornelius story (15:14) is the proof that the restoration of the fallen house of David has already occurred as well as the Gentiles' seeking the Lord. Luke has James express a very old conception of mission: the conversion of Gentiles is the fulfilment of the promises to Israel. It does not mean that the promises given to Israel have been transferred to the Gentiles, while Israel has been excluded, but that the Gentiles have gained a share in what has been given to Israel. This fits with Jewish expectation that at the end of times Gentiles will be included in the restored Israel.

The conversion and restoration of Israel is the basis for the Gentiles' seeking the Lord, and so the missionaries operate in synagogues with their mixed audiences. Conversion occurs via the synagogue, because here the scattered of the Dispersion are gathered, because the inclusion of the unrepentant must take place here and because here you find the Gentiles. The streaming in of Gentiles, described in Acts as conversions in connection with Jewish conversions, reveals who really belongs to Israel. Luke's version of 'the Jew first', then, is determined by the idea that without 'the Jew first' the Gentiles would have no admission to salvation.

The Gentiles' sharing in the promises to Israel is something more than a historically necessary event, as it is commanded by God in the Scriptures (Luke 24:47; Acts 3:25; 13:47; 15:16f., cf. 10:43). But Gentiles only appear after the restoration of Israel. The resurrected Lord revealed to the apostles the key to understanding the Scriptures (Luke 24:45ff.): the Scriptures witness to the crucifixion and the resurrection of the Messiah, *and* 'that repentance and forgiveness of sins should be preached in his name to all nations, beginning from Jerusalem'; in Acts, 'the nations' (*ta ethnē*) are the non-Jewish peoples. The mission solely to Jews, from the beginning in Jerusalem, does not mean a restriction of salvation to Jews, but to Israel, as the peoples must be reached through Israel and become associated with Israel. The mission to the Gentiles is simply a part of the mission to the Jews. The command to world mission in Acts 1:8 shows the disciples witnessing in Jerusalem, Judaea and Samaria, and to the ends of the earth. 'To the ends of the earth' does not mean the Gentile mission: throughout Acts the mission goes from synagogue to synagogue, ending with a meeting with the Jews in Rome (28:17ff.). There is no specific mission to the Gentiles, separated from the mission to the Jews. It is striking that in their speeches to Jews the apostles emphasize the sharing of the Gentiles in salvation, while in their speeches to Gentiles, they mention their commission to Israel.[62] In Peter's speech at the house of the Gentile Cornelius (10:34–43) the introductory statement (vv. 34f.) shows that the occasion is significant for the history of mission. However, the essential body of the sermon (vv. 35–43) makes no reference to this situation: the Jesus-event is described as taking place solely within a Jewish framework; the people to whom the witnesses shall preach (10:42) is Israel. In the important first speech to Gentiles, Peter discusses the salvation that has come to Israel. The message to Israel also includes Gentiles, who can be reached only through Israel, and that the gospel is for all people is repeatedly stressed to Jews. In his speech to Jews from all over the world present in Jerusalem (2:14–40), Peter says that the promise is 'to you and your children and to all that are far off': in light of Luke 24:47 and Acts 1:8, the passage can only be understood as indicating the inclusion of Gentiles in the promises to Israel. In the speech in 3:11–26, with a discussion of the meaning of the Jewish decision for or against the call to repentance, the message has a further address beyond the Jews: to you *first* it has been preached (v. 26). The quotation from Genesis 22:18 in v. 25, 'and by your descendants (*sperma*) shall all the nations of the earth find blessing', means that the salvation comes through Israel, the addition of Gentiles is a part of the fulfilment of the promises to Israel. This is because *to sperma Abraam* in Luke's writings never refers to Christ, but to Israel and the Israelites (Luke

---

[62] There is no missionary speech in Acts aimed only at Gentiles; the missionaries meet the Gentiles always when they meet Jews, hence the synagogue scenes. And even when Paul is being excluded from a synagogue or leaves it, he continues with his mission to the Jews in the same city: 18:6ff.

1:55; Acts 7:5–6; 13:23, cf. Luke 13:16; 19:9). The 'seed' is made up of the repentant portion of the people.

In the only missionary speech of Paul (13:16–41),[63] it is emphasized repeatedly that the promises belong to Jews and that salvation has been sent to them (vv. 23,26,31,33), and to the Jews it is said that everyone who believes in Christ is justified (v. 39). That means, according to vv. 40f.,46ff., that justification also includes Gentiles, who share in salvation. A great number of Jews and proselytes are converted, while others reject the gospel (v. 46).[64] And then the time has come, when they have judged themselves unworthy of the salvation of Israel, to offer a share in salvation to the Gentiles. The Jews are divided into two camps through the missionary preaching, by means of which the repentant are separated from the others. It is necessary to clarify who belongs to Israel. The mission ends in Rome (Acts 28:23ff.): Acts closes with a description of a people divided over the Christian message, some believing, others unbelieving (v. 24). To the unbelieving portion Paul in vv. 26f. applies Isaiah 6:9f., as a judgement on the hardened.

The gospel has reached the ends of the earth and the world mission among Jews is completed. Upon those who have been converted the promises have been fulfilled. They are the cornerstone of the true Israel into which the Gentiles have now been incorporated.

In what way do the Gentiles receive a share in the promises to Israel? In the account of the Apostolic Council in Jerusalem (15:1–35), the Cornelius incident functions as proof (vv. 6ff.). The problem is not the Gentiles' sharing in salvation, their admission as such, but the conditions for their entrance. Peter had learned from the Cornelius-event that the Gentiles will be saved, in just the same way as the Jews (15:11). The proof for this is that God bestows the gift of the Spirit, which is the

---

[63] 14:14–18 is not a missionary *speech*, and 17:16–34 is not a *missionary* sermon, but an *apologetic* one.

[64] The passage does not mean that the Gentile mission appears to be a result of Jewish disobedience. The Gentile mission is justified, therefore, by a reference to prophecy, Isa. 49:6. And the declaration in v. 46 does not mean the end of the mission to the Jews, because Luke goes on to describe their preaching in the synagogues (14:1; 17:1,10,17; 18:4,19; 19:8,26).

promise and property of Israel (Acts 2:17ff.), on Gentiles in the same way as on believing Jews (15:8–9). Yet as Gentiles they are unclean: this the Cornelius-event, with Peter's vision, has not changed. As a substitute for Jewish membership in the people of God, God accepts as valid the cleansing that has come upon them by faith (15:9). They are saved as Gentiles without circumcision, that is without first becoming proselytes. No annulment of the privileged position of Israel is meant; that is shown in the speech of James, with its quotation from Amos 9:11f. in 15:13ff. The speech presupposes the connection with Israel, though without the Jewish observance of the law and without Jewish status. It is clear that the Jews in the church keep the law (21:20); this even distinguishes them from the unbelieving Jews. And they keep the law as this makes it clear that the church is Israel – the Torah is the distinguishing mark of Israel. Not, as even Jews know, that there is any salvation through fulfilling the law. The situation for the Gentiles in the church – and they remain Gentiles – is different: they only have to keep that part of the law which according to the Scriptures is necessary for Gentiles. This is the idea behind the Apostolic Decree (15:20,29; 21:25). To Luke the Decree is a part of the Mosaic law (v. 21), namely the part related to foreigners living together with Israelites (Lev. 17:10ff.). The main idea of the law, according to Luke, is the first commandment, namely to confess God as the one God, which is against idolatry. Further to this, Gentiles keep some few commandments in order not to defile the Israelites. Israel is really the Jewish people, that is the repentant ones, the Jewish Christians, who formed the nucleus of the church.

THE PEOPLE OF THE SPIRIT

In the church you find the 'sons of the prophets' (Acts 3:25). Where the Spirit is, there is the people of God. It has always been so in the history of Israel, still is so today and will be in the future until the end of times.

It is decisive for Luke that the Spirit is God's Spirit. Luke speaks in Acts mostly of 'the Holy Spirit' (39), sometimes merely of 'the Spirit' (11) or 'the Spirit of the Lord' (2).[65] The Spirit's relation to God as his Spirit is seen by the fact that the Spirit is there before Christ as God's active and prophetic presence with his people. Further, the Spirit is referred to as 'the Father's promise' (Acts 1:4; Luke 24:49). Above all, in Acts 2:33, Jesus 'having been exalted to the right hand of God, received from the Father the promised Holy Spirit and poured it out': the role and position of the Messiah is given through God anointing him with the Holy Spirit (Acts 10:38; Luke1:35; 4:18).

The Spirit is an impersonal,[66] active force, God's creative and prophetic presence in the history of the people. No wonder that Luke, more than any other New Testament author, depicts the Spirit as it appears in the Old Testament: the Spirit inspires prophecy (Num. 24:2; 1 Sam. 11:6; 2 Sam. 23:2; 2 Chr. 24:20; Neh. 9:30; Joel 3:2; Hos. 9:7; Zech. 7:1f.); raises up leaders (Judg. 6:34; 11.29; Isa. 11:1–5); creates heaven and men (Ps. 33:6; Jdt. 16:14; Job 33:4); judges and purifies (Isa. 4:4), and, in all this and above all, God pours out his Spirit on Israel (Isa. 44:3; 59:21; Ezek. 36:27; 37:14; 39:29; Joel 3:1ff.; Hag. 2:5; Zech. 12:10).

For Luke the Spirit belongs to Israel and is part of the history of the people of God. The Spirit has not appeared for the first time with Jesus or the church: it has always been there, but is an essential part of Israel in the end-time, the church. And so the restoration of Israel is seen as the work of the Spirit (Acts 1:1 – 2:42). The main themes in the proem (1:1–8) are the kingdom (1:3,6), the Spirit (1:4,5,8) and the witness to the ends of the earth (1:8). The restoration of the kingdom is its restoration to Israel (1:6).[67] The answer to the apostles' question about restoring the kingdom to Israel is that the Spirit will come upon them and they will be witnesses from Jerusalem to 'the end of the earth' (1:8). This is a part of the restoration, so the witness of 1:8 is primarily a witness to Israel (2:14,22,36,39; 3:13,25;

[65]   There are two exceptions to this: Acts 2:17, 'my [God's] Spirit', and Acts 16:7, 'the Spirit of Jesus'.

[66]   Only exceptionally does Luke attribute to it personal actions: Acts 16:7; Luke 2:26.

[67]   On the combination of Spirit and kingdom see J.D.G. Dunn, 'Spirit and Kingdom', *ET* 82, 1970–1, 36–40; S.S. Smalley, 'Spirit, Kingdom, and Prayer in Luke–Acts', *NTS* 15, 1973, 63f. Acts 1:6 is no nationalistic misunderstanding.

4:8,10; 5:12ff.,29ff.; 7; 10:36,42; 11:19; 13:16ff.; 14:1ff.; 16:12ff.; 17:1ff.,10ff.; 18:4ff.,24ff.; chapters 22–8). The kingdom of Israel is seen even in 1:15–26, the restoration of the leadership of the people. Luke sees the leader of the people replaced after the old ones had failed, not least by opposing the Spirit (Acts 7:51–3). This restoration is part of the work of the Spirit (1:6). The link between the Spirit and Israel is further seen in the outpouring of the Spirit (Acts 2).

The first recipients of the Spirit are all Jews, above all the twelve apostles (2:4,14). The audience on the day of Pentecost consists only of Jews (2:5,14b,22). The Spirit is offered to the people of the Spirit, Israel; to this people belongs the promise (2:33,39), and this promise is nothing but the Spirit (Acts 1:4,8; Luke 24:49). The christology of Acts 2 carries the theme further: the exaltation of Jesus is his enthronement, that is on the throne of David (Acts 2:30–3). The messiahship of Jesus is determined by his being anointed by God with the divine Spirit, and this has happened for the children of Israel (10:36,38). The exalted Messiah, sitting on the throne of David, receives and pours out the Spirit (2:33,39).

The idea of the Spirit as the distinguishing mark of the people of God permeates the whole of Acts. Stephen is characterized by an irresistible Spirit (6:5,10; 7:55), and it is therefore absurd to accuse him of speaking against Israel, that is against the law, the temple and Moses (6:11,13,14; 7:51–3). The Spirit is especially connected with the temple (Luke 1–2), the law (Luke 1–2; Acts 7:53) and Moses, who is a prophet and miracle-worker (7:36–7,38; 3:22; 6:11,14; 13:49 etc.).

The combination Spirit–Israel is seen also in the notion, according to Luke, that the Spirit always has been active in the history of Israel. The Gentiles receive the Spirit which is the property of Israel and so they share the promises to the people of God. That the Spirit always has been there in the history of Israel is implied already in the relation of the Spirit to God as 'the Father's promise' (Acts 1:4; 2:33; Luke 24:49). Further, Luke relates the Spirit to the prophecy of Joel 3:1–2 (Acts 2:17ff.), and it is asserted explicitly in Acts 7:51, where Luke sees the history of God's people as a history of resistance and opposition to the Spirit. The difference between the time of Israel before and after Jesus is not the difference between a time with and a time without the Spirit, but between different attitudes to the Spirit. Israel has always, throughout the history of the people, repudiated the Spirit (Acts 7:51). The fathers resisted the Spirit by killing the prophets, and the greatest of the prophets is Moses (Acts 7:17–41). His lawgiving is mentioned only in passing (7:38), whereas he is seen above all as the great prophet of Israel (Acts 7:36ff., cf. 3:22), who proclaimed the coming of the 'Righteous one' (Acts 7:52b). And the coming of the 'Righteous one', the Messiah, means the restoration of the kingdom to Israel (1:6). The Spirit is the promise, the restoring energy of God in rebuilding Israel.

The Spirit, active in the history of Israel, is the power which has called the holy Scriptures into being; the Spirit speaks in the Scriptures (Acts 1:16; 4:25; 28:25). God's words in the Scriptures are the words of the Spirit; when the people have the Scriptures, they have the Spirit among them. The words of the Spirit in the Scriptures were first and foremost prophetic sayings, about Judas and the Twelve on Israel's thrones, the opposition from Israel and the Gentiles to Jesus, the hardening of Israel (1:16; 4:25ff.; 28:26f.), and the words of the Spirit are the gospel, which you can find verbatim in the Scriptures (Acts 3:18ff.; 13:29; 26:22–3; 28:23; Luke 24:45–7).

Israel is disobedient to the Spirit, which means it is disobedient to the Scriptures (Acts 13:27). There is no ambiguity in the Scriptures, as they speak openly and clearly. The church adds nothing to what has already been written by Moses and the prophets.[68] There has been no time in the history of Israel when the people have been without prophets. They can listen to the gospel of the Messiah, his death and resurrection, on the sabbath in the synagogue (Acts 13:27).[69] The Spirit is linked with Israel and the prophets, and so to the Messiah of

[68] Luke has no idea of a veil upon the Scriptures or upon the heart of the readers, so that they cannot understand them (2 Cor. 3:12–18), and there are no hidden mysteries (1 Cor. 2:6ff.).

[69] The meaning is not that they did not know the words of the prophets, but that they did not know Jesus, that is, they did not understand that he was the one the Scriptures were all about.

Israel.[70] In Luke 1–2 a group of people act as prophets and introduce the coming Messiah of Israel before and after his advent (1:41–5,47–55,67–80; 2:25–32,36–8).[71] The Baptist, too, is a prophet (1:67,76). The main idea in the proem is that the coming of the Messiah means the restoration of the Israel of God and the fulfilling of the promises (Luke 1:16–17,32f.,51–5, 68–79; 2:10–11,25–32,38). Luke 1–2 is, so to say, the 'missing link' between the prophets of old, the prophet Jesus and the prophets of the church. The task of the prophets at the stage of prophecy in Luke 1–2 is to tell who the Messiah is, to identify him; the Spirit has been a part of the history of Israel, and a new wave of prophets shows up in order to introduce the Messiah-Jesus. In Acts 2 Luke does not introduce something new and unheard of in the history of the people; he uses the Scriptures (Joel 2:28ff.). Luke is out to identify and legitimate what happened on Pentecost: a new outburst of the Spirit on Israel.[72] The Spirit is not there constantly in the church and not at the church's disposal. It is a gift coming down from heaven, *ubi et quando visum est deo.* The church is the true Israel in so far as Christians obey the Spirit (Acts 7:51; 5:32). The true Israel no longer opposes the Spirit as Israel has done in the past (Acts 7:51). Any opposition to the Spirit within the church means death to the persons in question (Acts 5:1–11).

Luke gives us the history of prophecy in Israel. The first step is the word about the coming Messiah, the one to save, restore and rebuild the people of God. This is the Alpha and the Omega of the Scriptures. *All* the prophets have spoken about

[70] It is well known that the eschatological time of salvation in Jewish thought is determined by a particular display of God's power by the Spirit: Joel 2:28–9; Ezek. 36:26; 4 Ezra 13; Test. Levi 18.

[71] Cf. A. George, 'L'esprit saint dans l'oeuvre de Luc', *RB* 85, 1978, 514, n.38; G.H.W. Lampe, *The Holy Spirit in the Writings of St Luke*, Oxford 1955, 160; J.A. Fitzmyer, *The Gospel According to Luke* I, 229; G. Friedrich, προφήτης', *TDNT* VI, 835f.

[72] The answer to the question about the difference between Acts 2 and the former activity of the Spirit is that before Jesus the Spirit was given only to some few prophets and sporadically, but now to all members of the church. Luke does not say anything about the frequency of the Spirit's activity before Jesus, but Acts 7:51–3 would more easily be understood to mean that the Spirit had spoken frequently to the people. Nowhere in Acts do we find that all people of the church are characterized as prophets or guided by the Spirit of prophecy.

the coming of a suffering and exalted Messiah (Luke 24:25–7,44; Acts 3:18ff.,24; 10:43; 13:27–9; 24:14; 26:22). The next step in history is what may be called the last prophets before Christ, who at the time of his coming proclaim him as the promised Messiah (Luke 1–2). The third step we have after Easter and Pentecost: the prophets through the Spirit testify that Messiah has come, and that the crucified, resurrected and exalted Jesus is the promised Messiah of Israel (Acts 2:29ff.; 7:55–6; 10:38; 17:2–3).

That the Spirit is an inherent part of the history of the people of God is seen even in the rare sayings about the outpouring of the Spirit on the Gentiles. In the first part of Acts, chapters 1–15, a clear impression is given of the charismatic, Spirit-filled life of the church in Jerusalem.[73] When it comes to Gentiles, we have but one scene which tells us about the outpouring of the Spirit on non-Jews (Acts 10:44f.,47; 11:15; 15:8).[74] Luke is restrictive when it comes to the Spirit and the Gentiles. The mission to the Gentiles is not an invention of the church or the apostles, but solely the responsibility of God and the Spirit. This is clear from the story about Cornelius in Acts 10–11 and in its echo in Acts 15:7–9,14; God forces a reluctant Peter into missionary effort among Gentiles. In this context we have no fewer than six sayings about the outpouring of the Spirit on Gentiles (10:44,45,47; 11:15,16; 15:8). It is unprecedented that non-Jews receive the gift which belongs solely to Israel, and Luke stresses this as a miracle (10:45,47; 11:15; 15:8–9). The gift of the Spirit is the sign that even Gentiles shall be saved (11:18; 15:8). The Spirit does not create a new Israel, something like a 'third race', but God's work through the Spirit has the outcome that even Gentiles become members of the people of God, Israel. When Luke emphasizes the connection between Israel

---

[73]   In Acts 1–15 we find forty-five instances out of a total of fifty-seven in Acts. Most of the few sayings in Acts 16–28 deal with Paul and his last journey to Jerusalem (Acts 16:6–7; 19:2,6,21; 20:22,23,28; 21:4,11; 28:25).

[74]   As for Acts 8:4–25, the Samaritans are not seen as Gentiles: J. Jervell, *People of God*, 113–32; R.J. Coggins, 'The Samaritans and Acts', *NTS* 28, 1982, 423–34. The Spirit's activity in Antioch (Acts 13:2) concerns a mixed congregation, above all active in the mission to the Jews in the Dispersion; Acts 19:6 refers to Jews, that is to former disciples of the Baptist.

and the Spirit and shows that the Spirit always has been a part of the history of Israel, he demonstrates the continuity between the church and Israel. Where the Spirit is, there you find the people of God.

The Jews in Jerusalem are named 'the sons of the prophets' (Acts 3:25).[75] According to Acts 7:52 the inhabitants of Jerusalem have already rejected the preaching of the apostles and killed the Prophet, Jesus, and so they are merely the sons of the murderers of the prophets. The idea of the Jews as murderers of the prophets is known to the New Testament writers (Matt. 5:12; 23:30f.; Heb. 11:33–8; James 5:10): only Luke sees the Jews as 'sons of the prophets'; this means that they are heirs of the promises, the salvation, foretold by the prophets in the Scriptures (Acts 3:24,25b, cf. 13:32).

When Luke uses the term 'prophet', he means the prophets in the Scriptures and Christ as the promised prophet (Acts 3:22f.; 7:38); the prophets in the church are mentioned only at 11:27; 13:1; 15:32; and 21:9f. The scriptural prophets and the ones in the church stem from the same Spirit. The gospel is given verbatim in the prophetic writings in the Scriptures (Luke 24:25–7,44–7; Acts 3:17ff.,25ff.; 4:24–6; 7(*passim*); 8:32–5; 10:43; 13:27,34ff.; 17:2–3; 26:22; 28:23).[76] The gospel not only corresponds with the Scriptures, but its content is also derived and drawn from the Scriptures. Luke underlines that 'everything' in the Jesus story is already written down (Luke 18:31; Acts 4:24–6). Paul himself does not say anything apart from what 'the prophets and Moses' already have said, which is written down (Acts 26:22). The Scriptures contain everything that the church preaches. Therefore the benevolent Jews in Beroea turn to the Scriptures in order to find and confirm the gospel there (Acts 17:11). The gospel is there already in the synagogue, in the reading from the Scriptures (Luke 4:16ff.; Acts 13:15,27).

Jesus' messianic status is declared by reading the Scriptures in the synagogue (Luke 4:16ff.). The Ethiopian eunuch can read and understand what Isaiah 53:7–8 is all about; the

---

[75] There are no parallels to this expression within the New Testament, and there are no parallels in early Judaism.

[76] We have the gospel without any reference to the Scriptures in Acts 4:10 and 5:30.

content is clear, the problem is the identity of the person
mentioned by the prophet (Acts 8:32–5). When Paul declares
the gospel to Herod Agrippa, the problem is whether the king
believes the prophets or not (26:27). The 'opening' of the
Scriptures (Luke 24:32,45; Acts 17:3) is simply the identification
of Jesus as the Messiah. The Spirit does not give the church
the words of the gospel, as these are already given by the
Spirit in the Scriptures.

There is a connection between Spirit and preaching; this
does not concern the content, but the way the words of the
gospel are preached. The preaching is done 'with boldness'.
This 'freedom of speech' in Acts has only to do with preaching
(2:29; 4:13,29,31; 9:27,28; 13:46; 14:3; 18:26; 26:26; 28:31). The
'boldness' concerns situations when the apostles are threatened,
persecuted, in court, prisoners: that is in dangerous situations.
Regularly the 'boldness' confronts a hostile audience or pub-
licity. This manner of speaking serves to demonstrate the
proclamation of the word of God. The 'boldness' is not a
question of personal qualities, but is a gift of the Spirit. Further,
the connection between Spirit and word is given in the miracles
accompanying the preaching.[77] In the prayer of Acts 4:24–30,
the members of the congregation request God to enable them
to speak with 'boldness' while God causes healings and signs
and miracles to happen through the name of Jesus; the
wonders are the work of the Spirit (4:33). The apostles
witnessed the resurrection of Jesus with 'great power'. The
preaching is confirmed by the miracles, and God testifies to his
word by miracles and signs (Acts 5:32; 6:3,5; 8:29,39; 13:12;
14:3; 19:10–11). The speaking in tongues, the glossolalia, is an
attendant circumstance, accompanying prophecy (Acts 2:4;
10:46; 19:6); speaking in tongues and prophecy are interpreted
as the outpouring of the Spirit (2:4,17a,18b). Speaking in
tongues, as well as prophecy, come from the Spirit, but they
are not identical phenomena; glossolalia accompanies prophecy, that is preaching.

The Spirit utters words, but these spoken words are never the

---

[77]   For the miracles in Acts: J. Jervell, *Unknown Paul*, 77–95.

gospel or the word of God. Its words are the word of God only when they come from the Spirit as the one speaking in the Scriptures (Acts 1:16; 4:25; 28:25). Apart from these instances the words uttered by the Spirit are all sorts of words and commands affecting the life of the church, from 'commonplaces' to prophecy of a coming starvation, 'words for the moment' (8:29; 10:19f.; 11:28; 13:2; 15:28; 20:23; 21:4,11; 23:9).[78] The main idea is that the Spirit is the Spirit of prophecy as it testifies in various ways to the words of the Scriptures: these words are infallible, whereas Paul can refuse to obey the words of the Spirit when they come to him from the prophets in the church (Acts 21:24).[79] Still the Spirit-prophecies[80] of the church serve to demonstrate that the church is the people of the God of Israel. The church does not lead and guide itself: God does through the Spirit, voices, visions etc. Therefore the Spirit as a rule acts and speaks directly from heaven (1:5ff.; 2:4ff.,33,38; 4:8,31; 5:32; 6:3,5,10; 8:29,39; 9:31; 10:19; 11:24,28; 13:2ff.,9,52; 15:28; 16:6,7; 19:21; 20:22f.,28; 21:4,11).[81] It may be correct to say that the 'Spirit is given only when the Twelve are present or a member or a delegate of the Twelve is on the scene',[82] but then the idea is that of the people of God, not of an intermediary office.

These prophecies separate the church from the synagogue; such prophecies do not occur outside of the church. Other prophets are mentioned, but these are false prophets or magicians (Acts 8:9–11; 13:6,8; 19:13–17). Visions and prophetic words are never described as occurring in the synagogue, because its

---

[78] We have in Acts several occurrences of similar words, but they differ from the ones above with respect to the source of the words, angels (5:19; 8:26; 10:3,22; 11:7f.; 23:23f.); *kyrios* (9:9,10f.; 18:9; 22:19; 23:11); voice (from heaven) (10:13ff.; 11:7ff.; 22:7ff.).

[79] When, in spite of the words of the Spirit, Paul goes to Jerusalem, he shows an unprecedented attitude towards the prophecies in the Scriptures. There is a great difference!

[80] The fact that the Spirit speaks, utters words, is not enough to characterize the Spirit as person or personal, because the words are sometimes uttered by the prophets in the church and their 'ego' is naturally possessed by the Spirit when they speak to the church.

[81] Very seldom the Spirit is given or comes by the means of human instruments, an office in the church, or apostles: 8:15ff.; 9:17; 10:44; and 19:6.

[82] J.A. Fitzmyer, *The Gospel According to Luke* I, 231.

members do not obey the prophets, and so do not have the Spirit of prophecy and will be expelled from the people (3:22–3). Members of the church, by contrast, are the true 'sons of the prophets' and the 'sons of the covenant' given to Abraham (3:25). Prophecy is the expression of continuity in the history of Israel.

The contrast between 'letter' and 'Spirit' is essential in Paul's preaching (Rom. 2:29; 7:6; 2 Cor 3:6ff.; Gal. 3:2–4; Phil. 3:3). The Spirit came to the world with Christ (Gal. 4:6). Luke, on the other hand, not only sees the Spirit as an active force in the history of Israel, but combines Pentecost and law.[83] Luke is fully aware of Pentecost as a Jewish festival (Acts 20:16). Paul goes to Jerusalem in order to take part in Jewish ceremonies (Acts 24:11,12,17f.). Luke knows of sacrifices and almsgiving as important elements in the law of Moses,[84] and Paul's journey to Jerusalem to fulfil the law is 'arranged' by the Spirit. The outpouring of the Spirit is combined with a Jewish festival, and so it is clear even here that the Spirit is an occurrence within the history of Israel.

Luke's point of view is that the Spirit leads to obedience to the law of Moses, and, because the church has the Spirit and obeys the law, this church is Israel. But the unfaithful part of the people opposes the Spirit and does not keep the law (Acts 7:51–3). There are no tensions within the Scriptures; the law contains prophecy as well as commandments;[85] Luke shows from the beginning of his work the harmony between Spirit and law (Luke 1–2). The coming of the Messiah of Israel is proclaimed by an outburst of the Holy Spirit, expressed in prophecy, which centres on the identity and task of the Messiah (Luke 1:4ff.,46ff.,59,67ff.; 2:25–32,36ff.). At the same time the

---

[83] This does not mean that he regarded Pentecost as the feast for the giving of the law at Sinai. We do not know when the festival of Pentecost come to commemorate the giving of the law at Sinai. This might have been the case long before Luke wrote; so E. Schweizer, 'πνεῦμα', *TDNT* VI, 408f. The outpouring of the Spirit at Pentecost is no contrast to or correlative of the giving of the law at Sinai; against E. Haenchen, *Acts*, 175ff.; W. Knox; E. Lohse, 'πεντηκοστή', *ThWNT* VI, 46–9.

[84] J. Jervell, *People of God*, 140.

[85] On the law as prophecy see Luke 24:27,44; Acts 3:22; 7:35ff.; 24:14; 26:22; 28:23; on ceremonial aspects: Luke 2:21,22,23,24,27,39; 5:14; 20:28; Acts 6:14; 7:8; 15:1,5; 18:15; 21:21; 22:3 etc.

law-observant people performs for this Messiah, who is created by the Spirit (Luke 2:21ff.,27,37,39,41ff.), what is required by the law. Israel, with its centre in the temple of Jerusalem, is the setting for the Messiah (Luke 1:16,32,33,54,55,68–79,80; 2:10, 11,22,25,32,41ff.). There are parallels between Spirit and law (Acts 7:51–3). The church has Spirit and law; the synagogue has the law, but does not keep it (Acts 7:53; 15:21). Moses is the charismatic prophet, miracle-worker and lawgiver (Acts 3:22; 6:11,14; 7:36–8). The central thrust of the law according to Acts is the struggle against idolatry, above all in the first commandment about the one and only God of Israel. When Israel does not obey Moses and the law from Sinai, they turn to other gods (7:40ff.); they are uncircumcised, that is they act as Gentiles (7:39,51;[86] 4:27–8) – circumcision is the sign of Israel as the people of God (Luke 2:21; Acts 7:8; 15:1,5; 21:21). When the Jews reject the Spirit and the law, they are no longer Israel and God's people. Stephen is accused of speaking against the law, and at the same time he is a charismatic prophet (Acts 6:11, 13–14, cf. 6:3,4,8,10; 7:55).

They who have the Spirit, keep the law;[87] this was so not only at the dawn of the coming of the Messiah (Luke 1–2). Luke regards Jesus as one who kept the law (Acts 6:13–14; the witnesses are false); this in turn determines the presentation of Jesus in the Gospel. The Christians obviously have no problems in keeping the law: the whole church in Jerusalem is guided by the Spirit (1:8; 2:4,17ff.,38; 4:8,31; 5:31ff.; 6:3ff.); at the same time it lives according to the law (Acts 10:14,28; 11:3ff.,8; 21:21). Paul is the prophetic charismatic, who has always kept the law and keeps it today, performing even more than the law requires (16:3; 18:18; 21:20–6; 22:3; 23:1–5; 24:11f,14,17,18; 26:5; 28:17); all charges against Paul of breaking the law are shown to be false (21:21,24,28; 28:18). On the other hand, even the high priest does not keep the law (23:3), and this is said generally about all

---

[86] The commentaries in general notice that Spirit and law are mentioned together, without any attempt to explain the relation between them and to Stephen's speech as a whole.

[87] In Judaism we have combined the eschatological outpouring of the Spirit and the complete obedience to the law (so e.g. Test. Judah 24; Orac. Sibyl. 3:573; the Spirit and prophecy were given at Sinai according to Exodus Rabbah 5:12; 28:12.

unbelieving Jews (7:53); those who oppose the Spirit do not keep the law, but those who have received and obey the Spirit do. It is clear that for Luke the law does not give salvation. The Jews in the church keep the law as a whole, because after the outpouring of the Spirit there is in Israel no longer any disobedience to the law. The church consists of people 'zealous for the law' (Acts 21:21). Even when Luke deals with the Gentiles in the church he combines law, Spirit and Israel: the gift of the Spirit is given to the Gentiles (10:44–6; 11:15; 15:8) and so is the law, because the Apostolic Decree is part of the law, namely 'the essentials' (15:28), and the Holy Spirit and Moses are the authorities behind the decree (15:21,28). The Spirit gives those without the law ceremonial commandments and regulations.

For the people of the Spirit the law is no longer a burden. The believing Jews, among them Paul, keep the entire law, the Gentiles part of it. There is harmony between Spirit and law.

THE LAW

Luke refers repeatedly to Jews charging Christians with apostasy, with having abandoned the law: Jesus altered the law of Moses (Acts 6:14); Stephen made blasphemous statements against the law, that is against God (6:11,13); they amend the law; Paul invalidates the law, preaches apostasy from Moses and thus speaks against Israel (21:21,28; 25:8; 28:17). Luke rejects the accusations as baseless and false (6:11,13f.; 21:21ff.). At the same time he charges the Jews with not keeping the law and with rejecting Moses (7:35,39,53; 15:10; 23:3 etc.).

This is something far more to Luke than a description of something which happened in the church long before his own time, a purely historical matter.[88] The question of the law is a burning problem to him, and he returns to it again and again, for it has to do also with the identity of the church.[89]

---

[88]   The question of the law has been neglected for a long time. Luke was seen as a witness to the end of a process in early Christianity, namely the formation of the old catholic church, and consequently as a further development of Pauline ideas regarding the law: the law as an *adiaphoron*.

[89]   The question of the law in Luke–Acts has been dealt with, falsely, by contrasting

Luke has emphatically positive and consistent statements on the law: it consists of 'living words' (Acts 7:38), is of a divine nature, is delivered by angels (7:53), is eternally valid, not 'one stroke of a letter in the law' will be dropped (Luke 16:17). Luke's peculiar and characteristic interpretation of the significance of the law can be seen even in his terminology, which differs from other New Testament writers and from the apostolic fathers.

Luke alone employs terms like 'the law of the Lord' and 'the law of the fathers' (Acts 22:3; Luke 2:23,24,39).

He refers to the Mosaic law as 'the customs which Moses delivered to us' and similar expressions (Acts 6:14; 15:1; 21:21; 28:17).

Only Luke talks about 'Moses being preached' (Acts 15:21) and uses the word *paranomein*, 'transgress the law' (Acts 23:3).

Lukan phrases are 'the living words' (Acts 7:38) and 'to speak against Moses/the law' (Acts 6:11,13,14; 21:21,28; 25:8; 28:17).

The name 'Moses' referring to the law appears frequently in Luke–Acts, seldom in other writings (Acts 6:11; 15:1,21; 21:21; Luke 5,14; 16:19,31; 24:27).

The expression 'the law of Moses' is used by Luke five times; in all other New Testament writings three times (Acts 13:39; 15:5; 28:23; Luke 2:22; 24:44).

We have only partial parallels, mostly from Hellenistic Jewish sources: this is more Jewish than biblical phraseology.

The law remains for Luke the law given to Israel on Sinai, in the strict meaning of the word, the law of Israel. Luke is concerned about the law because it is Israel's law.[90] Significantly, Luke is most concerned about the ritual and ceremonial aspects of the law, for the law is to him not essentially the moral law, but the mark of distinction between Jews and non-Jews: the law is the sign of Israel as the people of God.

Luke with Paul with regard to soteriology; on the contrary, it has to do with ecclesiology.

[90] The conflicts within early Christianity over the law centred on the question of salvation, but concerned also the relationships to Israel and the 'self-understanding' of the church; see chapter 4, 'Acts and the New Testament'.

The heart of the law is circumcision (Acts 7:8; 15:1,5; 16:3; 21:21; Luke 2:21); Luke never spiritualizes or reinterprets this as is done elsewhere in the New Testament.[91] The life of the primitive church in Jerusalem as depicted in the early chapters of Acts is determined by universal adherence to the law, which is especially evident from the Christians' allegiance to the temple (Acts 1–7). Peter's and other Christians' allegiance to the law is essentially their obligation to ritual purity and consequently strict separation from the uncircumcised (Acts 10:13ff.,28; 11:3). The question of the law is the subject for the Apostolic Council (Acts 15:1ff.). All the ritual prescriptions in the law are performed by Jesus' parents (Luke 2:21,22,24,39.) Paul's whole pharisaic life up to his arrest in the temple is a demonstration of Jewish adherence to the law (16:3,13; 17:1,10; 18:4; 20:16; 21:21–6,28; 23:1,3,5,6; 24:14,17,18; 25:8; 26:4–5; 28:17). Jesus was an apprentice of the law, a rabbinic disciple in the temple (Luke 2:41ff.). It is significant that, in his Gospel, Luke avoids any criticism of the law by Jesus: he eliminates material dealing with controversies between Jesus and the Jewish leaders in matters of law, where Jesus opposes pharisaic interpretation (Matt. 5:17–20,21–48; 6:1–8,16–18; Mark 7:1–23). The explanation is to be found in Acts 6:14, 'the customs from Moses will be altered'; this notion is attributed to Jesus, but Luke sees it as patently false: therefore every criticism of the law is missing.[92] This is done deliberately in order to show the position of the Torah in the church. Jesus did not alter anything, the law is permanently valid.

Luke has no summary of the law in one central commandment, he does not in principle raise one commandment above others.[93] In the rewriting of Mark 12:28 in Luke 10:25ff., Luke points out that there is nothing like the first or great commandment; every commandment is as important as the rest. There is nothing like 'weightier matters of the law' (Matt. 23:23), but the

---

[91] Rom. 2:29; Phil. 3:3; Col. 2:11. Acts 7:51 represents no reinterpretation.
[92] The deletion of the material is mostly explained by the Gentile-Christian destination of Luke's writings. If so, much of Acts become enigmatic, e.g. the law-observant Jewish Pharisee Paul, the significant role of the matter of purity in Acts, and the Christians depicted as 'zealous for the law' (Acts 21:21).
[93] Matt. 7:12; 22:24–30; Mark 12:28ff.; Rom. 13:8ff.; Gal. 5:14.

law consists of giving tithes *and* care for justice and love (Luke 11:37–41). Love is not conceived as far more than sacrifices (Mark 12:33). In Luke's treatment of Mark's pericope on divorce (Luke 10:1–12), he avoids the obvious renunciation of Moses. There is no new interpretation of the law or the will of God by Jesus, no higher righteousness; the law is perfect and perpetually valid (Luke 16:17). The section about ritual cleanliness (Mark 7:1–23) is missing in Luke, even if Luke knew the Marcan record (cf. Luke 11:37ff.). There is no rejection of God's commandments 'in order to maintain the tradition of men' (Mark 7:8; Matt. 15:3ff.); on the contrary, Luke asserts the 'customs of the fathers', which are in harmony with the law (Acts 6:14; 21:21; 28:17, cf. 10:14ff.). The Christians' Jewish manner of life is in accordance with the law (Acts 1–7). In the rewriting of Matthew 23:25 (about the cleansing of cups and plates) in Luke 11:39ff., Luke gives the saying a Jewish flavour; almsgiving is important, and only he, among the New Testament writers, sees it as a sign of true adherence to the law and a duty to Israel (Luke 11:41; 12:33; Acts 9:36; 10:2,4,31; 24:17). Luke records no fewer than four disputes about the sabbath (Luke 6:1–5,6–11; 13:10–17 and 14:1–6); they do not show that the law is outdated and surpassed.[94] He is concerned to show that Jesus acted in complete accordance with the law, and that the Jewish leaders were not able to raise any objections. The Christian way of practising the sabbath is in accordance with Jewish rules: it is impossible for Luke to say that 'the sabbath was made for men' or that the saving of life allows for a transgression of the command – to free an Israelite on the sabbath (Luke 13:10–17) is what the law demands.[95]

In the Jewish charges of apostasy against Christians (Acts 6:11,13,14; 21:21,28; 25:8; 28:17), we have an indissoluble connection between Israel and the law. To sin against the law

---

[94] So S. Wilson, *Luke and the Law*, SNTSMS 50, Cambridge 1983, 27–43; 30: Luke 16:18 'challenges Mosaic authority'; but Luke 16:18 has a typically pharisaic extension of priestly regulations to the laity, and to demand stricter adherence to the law cannot mean to oppose it.

[95] There is no christological argumentation in these passages. And the missionary preaching in the synagogues, which cannot be separated from healing, is legitimate.

is to sin against Israel. And so we see the importance of the
conservative outlook: it is necessary that the Jewish Christians
keep the law and demonstrate its permanent validity, for there
is only one Israel, and all the promises are given to Israel. This
is emphasized in the exordium to the Gospel (Luke
1:16,30ff.,54–9, 69–75; 2:10f.,32–3 etc.), and it is reiterated in
the speeches in Acts (1:8; 2:26,39; 3:25; 13:26,32f.). God is the
God of Israel.

Abraham is the father of the people, and the figure is never
Christianized in Luke–Acts.[96] Abraham is the father of the
circumcised, not the father of uncircumcised Christians, and
the promises belong to Abraham and his children (Luke
1:68–75; Acts 3:25f.; 7:1,8). The law is the sign of the people of
God. The covenant given to Abraham is the covenant of
circumcision (Acts 7:8), which at the same time involves Gentile
participation in the promises to Israel (Acts 3:25; 15:16f.). Luke
attaches importance to the Mosaic law and stresses the Jewish
Christians as being zealous for the law; in this manner they
prove their identity as the people of God, entitled to salvation.
The mark of distinction between Christian Jews and other Jews
is not law or circumcision, rather it is that the Christian Jews
believe *all things* in the law and the prophets, which include the
acceptance of the crucified Messiah promised to the people and
now coming (Acts 24:14; 3:18,24; 10:43; Luke 18:31; 24:25,27,45).
Those who reject Jesus as the Messiah have lost their inheritance. Because Jewish Christians are the restored Israel, circumcision and law become the very marks of their identity. And
a considerable number of pious Jews have become Christians,
which is evident from the repeated mention of mass conversions
among Jews.

All the groups in the church have in the Torah one common
norm that guarantees the unity of the church. What about the
Gentiles and the law? The covenant of circumcision and the
promises to Israel involve the Gentiles' participation in Israel's
salvation (Acts 3:25; 13:47; 15:14–17; Luke 2:46–47); the people
of the circumcision and the law will be saved and 'a people

---

[96]   N.A. Dahl, 'The Story of Abraham in Luke–Acts', in L.E. Keck and J.L. Martyn
(eds.), *Studies in Luke–Acts*, New York 1966, 139ff.

from the Gentiles' will join Israel (Acts 15:14).[97] Luke labours to prove that the salvation of Gentiles occurs in complete accordance with the law. He offers the arguments in connection with the Apostolic Decree (15:20,29; 21:25). The very image in Acts of the Jewish-Christian church faithful to the law witnesses that the Apostolic Decree is neither an abrogation nor any new interpretation of the law. Some Jewish Christians from the pharisaic party demand from the Gentiles circumcision and keeping of the law (15:1,5); if the Gentiles do not fulfil these obligations, they cannot be saved. The meeting turns this down, as salvation comes through the grace of God (15:11). But Gentiles too have to keep the law, that is that part of the law which has to do with Gentiles living among Jews. The authority of the Council is not due to its apostolicity;[98] rather, according to Luke, it stems from James, the adherent of the law *par excellence*.[99] Scriptural proofs from the prophets ratify the admittance of Gentiles into the church (Acts 15:15ff.). Luke's general line of argument, however, is determined throughout by his appeal to the law *and* the prophets. In this case the actual proof comes from Moses and the law – this is clear from Acts 15:21, where we have a connection between Decree and law. The passage is seen as one of the most complicated in the New Testament, but the verse is complicated only if the Decree is understood as liberation from the law. Here it is said that the Decree is necessary because the law demands it; the Decree expresses what Moses demands from Gentiles in order that they may live among Israelites (Acts 15:15–17). The background is what Leviticus 17–18 demands from the 'strangers' in Israel.[100] The Decree is known from the synagogues as Moses is read there sabbath by sabbath, as happens all over the world. The Decree gives a common norm for Jews and Gentiles, grounding the unity of the church in the law. The main point in the Decree is that keeping the law, in this case the four command-

---

[97] Cf. N.A. Dahl, 'A People for His Name'.
[98] Against S. Wilson, *Luke and the Law*, 110: the decree is not Mosaic, but apostolic, and was by Luke's time a part of Christian mores, bound up with fundamental Hellenistic ethical principles.
[99] Cf. J. Jervell, *People of God*, 190–3.
[100] Themes from Lev. 17f. occur in several places in the Old Testament.

ments, is a confession of the one and only God of Israel. Therefore the commandments of purity are especially important, as the principles in the Decree show. As the Decree is part of the Torah, the law remains valid for both Jewish and Gentile Christians.[101]

Luke knows of no Gentile mission that is free from the law. He knows about a Gentile mission without circumcision, not without the law. The Decree enjoins Gentiles to keep that part of the law required for them to live together with Jews; it is not lawful to impose upon Gentiles more than Moses himself demanded. It is false to speak of the Gentiles as free from the law: the church, on the contrary, delivers the law to the Gentiles as Gentiles.[102] There is no justification by the law; rather it is by the grace of Jesus that Jews and Gentiles are saved (Luke 24:47; Acts 2:38; 3:19f.; 13:39; 15:11 etc.), but this is never contrasted with adherence to the law, otherwise Luke would have jeopardized his ecclesiology. It is impossible that the law should be abrogated, replaced, or conceived as belonging to an epoch now past. Therefore he disproves the Jewish accusations that the Christian Jews are taught by Paul to abandon circumcision and law (21:21,28; 25:8; 28:17f., cf. 6:11,13,14). The situation for Luke's church is clear. He opposes Jews who charge Christian Jews with apostasy from Israel, which would mean that these Christian Jews would not be entitled to salvation; this conflict is related to Paul, who is used as an argument against the church. At the time when Luke writes, the salvation of the Gentiles creates no problems for him: this matter has been settled. But the question about the law and Israel is acute,

---

[101]   Acts 13:38f. and 15:10f. are not inconsistent with my views. These passages have often been interpreted as law-critical, from the viewpoint of Paul and his understanding of the law. 13:38 shows the possibility of conversion, which includes the forgiveness of sins, which was not possible *en nomō Mōuseōs*. Nothing is said about the function and capability of the Torah; that the commandments and their fulfilling do not give salvation is known by the Jews too. Cf. K. Salo, 'Luke's Treatment of the Law. A Redaction-Critical Investigation', *AASF* 57, Helsinki 1991, 217; H. Räisänen, *Paul and the Law*, WUNT 29, Tübingen 1983, 94–119. Acts 15:10 does not say that the law cannot be kept in principle, but that the law *de facto* has not been kept, which in turn presupposes that it is possible to fulfil it. Cf. J. Nolland, 'A Fresh Look at Acts 15:10', *NTS* 27, 1980, 105,115.

[102]   H. Conzelmann, *Theology of St Luke*, 145ff. and 212f., asserts that the law is replaced by the Apostolic Decree; the law belonged to the old Israel.

because the Jewish element within the church is still a decisive factor. By insisting on Jewish Christians' observance of the law, he succeeds in showing that they are the restored and true Israel, entitled to God's promises and to salvation. The Jewish Christians' observance of the law, and the salvation of Gentiles as an associate people keeping parts of the law, are the distinguishing marks of the Israel that Moses and the prophets predicted as the people of the promises of salvation.

THE SCRIPTURES

The legitimacy of the church being Israel in the last phase of history can only be demonstrated by means of the Scriptures.[103] Luke's intention is clearly expressed through Paul's words in Acts 24:14: '[I believe] everything laid down by the law or written in the prophets'.

In various forms, 'everything' is a favourite term of Luke's, by which he often accents his claim to 'completeness' (Luke 1:3). He actually intends to omit nothing that Scripture offers.[104] Everything in the Old Testament is Scripture, everything is important, everything is binding. Luke is the fundamentalist within the New Testament. There is in Luke–Acts no criticism whatsoever of Scripture, such as we find in Matthew and Mark, not to mention Paul. Not even the idea that the Scriptures as a whole contain the promises whereas the gospel gives the fulfil-ment – which puts the Scriptures in a secondary position compared to the gospel – is present. Luke 16:16, 'until John it was the Law and the prophets; since that time the kingdom of God is preached . . .', cannot mean that once, long ago, we had an epoch with the law and the prophets, but they are not valid anymore.[105] The prophets have full authority in Acts; it cannot

---

[103] Luke's interpretation of Scripture: D. Bock, *Proclamation from Prophecy and Pattern. Lucan Old Testament Christology*, JSNTSS 17, Sheffield 1987; J. Jervell, *Unknown Paul*, 122–37; B.J. Koet, *Five Studies on Interpretation of Scripture in Luke–Acts*, SNTA 14, Leuven 1989.

[104] H. Conzelmann, *Theology of St Luke*, 158: for Luke 'Scripture' is not a title for the entire canon. But Luke's use of 'all' precisely implies what is later described as 'Scripture'.

[105] The meaning is simply that the proclamation of the gospel of the kingdom came after the Baptist.

be otherwise, as they also contain the gospel. Luke 16:17 confirms the unbroken validity and 'everlasting life' of the law of the Scriptures: 'It is easier for heaven and earth to come to an end than for one dot or stroke of the law to lose its force.'[106] Acts shows throughout the authority of the law.

We have no parallel in the New Testament to Luke's use of Scripture in Acts. This is evident in part from the standpoint of form. We note three different usages:

(1.) Direct quotations, especially to be found in the first part of Acts.

(2.) Summary references, where all that Scripture says is referred to (Acts 3:18,24; 10:43; 17:3; 18:28; 24:14; 26:23; Luke 24:25,46).

(3.) Recitals of narrative and indirect quotations in the two historical résumés (Acts 7:2–53 and 13:17–25).[107]

To the first form we have numerous parallels, but to the second only a very few.[108] The second form indicates that Luke regards Scripture in its totality; he does not speak of what one or a few of the prophets say, but is concerned with all the prophets (3:18,24; 10:43). In the New Testament only Luke speaks of 'all the prophets'; by this he understands all the Scriptures of the Old Testament, Moses, the prophets, the psalms and 'the writings'.

In his attempt to express in a summary form what Scripture says, Luke does not mean to extract an ideology from the Scriptures while ignoring other statements of the text. He does not speak of *the* Scripture, but collectively of 'the Scriptures' (17:2; 18:28) – not that Luke would have had a term such as 'Scripture' to express the collection of the various writings. Luke is the only writer in the New Testament who strives to show where in the Old Testament the authors quoted by him are to be found. He alone is aware of quoting from 'the book of Psalms' (Acts 1:20; cf. Luke 20:42–3), for this expression occurs

---

[106] This is not meant as irony, as some interpreters actually maintain.

[107] We have no parallel to this in the New Testament. Hebrews 11 is a collection of examples, whereas in Acts 7 and 13 a history as such is decisive.

[108] Matt. 22:40; 26:56; John 1:45; 5:39,46; 20:9; Rom. 1:2–3; 3:21; 16:26; 1 Cor. 15:3f.; Heb. 1:1.

only in Luke. He states that what is quoted is found in the second psalm (Acts 13:33), or that it appears 'in another place' (Acts 13:35). He speaks of 'the prophets' in general (Acts 3:18,24; 7:42; 10:43; 13:40; 15:15; 28:23), or of 'the prophet' (Acts 7:48), but he also mentions various prophets by name, thus Joel in Acts 2:17 and Isaiah in 28:16. He is interested in the identity of the author of an utterance in Scripture; this is especially true of David (Acts 1:16; 2:25,34; 4:25), but also of Moses (3:22; 7:37).

Very few of Luke's quotations and interpretations are drawn from tradition. Formal references, quotations and references to authors do not derive from tradition. This gives evidence of an independent study: Luke deduces his understanding of Scripture from study of the individual writing. He does not treat the Scripture *en bloc*, and he is concerned about the human agency of the word of God.

Scripture is to Luke an oral, spoken word. The Scripture is read aloud and publicly interpreted, not privately studied or read. Luke *can* introduce his quotations in Acts with the formula 'it is written' (1:20; 7:42; 13:33; 15:15), but this does not often happen.[109] He refers on twenty-two occasions to what has been 'spoken', 'said', 'commanded', 'preached' etc. He is the only one in the New Testament to speak of 'the mouth' of the prophets (3:18,21; 4:25; 13:27), or 'the voice' of the prophets. For good reasons the word of God in Scripture is for Luke a word which has been and shall be spoken, since the word is always a prophetic word, a word also heard weekly in the synagogue, and some members of the synagogue accept it (13:27; 15:21, cf. 2 Cor. 3:12–18).[110] God speaks in Scripture, above all through the prophets.

The centre of Scripture Luke locates in its prophetic aspect; this is true of the prophetic as phenomenon as well as of its content. The prophetic is to be found in all writings of

---

[109] Luke in the Gospel makes almost exclusive use of the expression 'it is written', owing to the dependence upon the tradition and the written Gospels Luke knew (Luke 1:1–4).

[110] The only parallel in the New Testament is the epistle to the Hebrews. The one who *speaks* in the Scriptures is God (Heb. 1:5ff.; 2:6,12; 4:3ff.; 5:5 etc.), in exceptional cases the Spirit (3:7,10,15), or David (4:7). Cf. B. Lindars, *The Theology of the Letter to the Hebrews*, NTT, Cambridge 1991, 50–5.

Scripture, in the writings of Moses as well as in the psalms and
the prophets. The summary scriptural references recapitulate
what Scripture says (Acts 3:18,24; 10:43; 17:3; 18:28; 24:14;
26:22; Luke 24:25,46). In three of the summaries 'the Scriptures'
are referred to (Acts 17:3; 18:28; Luke 24:46); the others, by
their more detailed definition of 'the Scriptures', indicate that
the term implies the prophetic element (Acts 3:18,24; 10:43;
24:14; 26:23; Luke 24:25–7). In these passages, reference is made
to the prophets; several times 'the law' or 'Moses' is added (Acts
26:22; Luke 24:27), in Luke 24:44 also 'the psalms'. The content
of all this is everywhere the same: the suffering and glory of
Christ.

The peculiar significance of the Scriptures and of the
prophetic is also expressed in the statement that the prophets
are present 'from of old'. God speaks through the prophets
who are 'from eternity' (Acts 3:21): this phrase does not refer
to time, but indicates that they are especially the words of
God; it is not the prophets who are from eternity, but God's
decision and measure. The context is the story of Christ,
especially the universal restoration through him; it is important
to show that this is not something new in Israel; it has been
there from the very beginning. Luke has a remarkable pre-
dilection for the old, the former things, the start: this is so that
he can show that the Christ-event was connected with Israel
from the beginning of history. The restoration of Israel and
the admittance of Gentiles to the people of God, described in
the Scriptures, is made known by God 'from eternity' (Acts
15:18), which comes from a quotation taken mainly from Amos
9:11f.; the word from the Scriptures, in this case the prophetic
word, is from eternity because it is God's word. The same is
true of the Law, as Moses 'of old times' is being preached in
the synagogues (Acts 15:21). An indirect connection with the
Scriptures is given in Acts 15:7: 'a long time ago' God chose
Peter as a missionary to the Gentiles; this 'a long time ago'
does not apply to the story about Cornelius, which has
recently happened, but to God's decision which took place
long ago and is even a part of Scripture. This gives expression
to a peculiar authority, God's own. Luke, and he alone in the

New Testament, characterizes the 'eternal' prophets as 'holy' (Acts 3:21, cf. Luke 1:70).

He cites only a very few of the writing prophets. He is not concerned with individual prophets and definitely not concerned with a selection, with 'testimonies', but speaks emphatically of 'all the prophets' (Acts 3:18,24; 10:43; Luke 24:27), or generally of 'the prophets' (Acts 3:21; 7:42,52; 13:27,40; 15:15; 26:22,27). At issue is the prophetic *per se*, that which in the genuine sense may be described as the word of God.

After Moses, David, the father of the Messiah, is the prophet *par excellence* in the Scriptures. David is important as the ancestor of Israel: he is *the* patriarch, and only he is given this title.[111] David is himself a writing prophet.[112] He is recognized as author of the psalms, which for this reason are described as prophetic writings (Acts 1:16; 2:25,34; 4:25; Luke 20:42–4, cf. Acts 2:30). David is the one through whom the Spirit speaks. Three times Luke writes that the Spirit is the one who speaks in Scripture, and in two of the passages David is the subject (Acts 1:16 and 4:25). The latter passage also implies that the speech of the Spirit is that of God, for God speaks through the Spirit and thus also through David. Scripture as words of the prophets throughout history is simply the word of the Spirit. This explains why the Spirit, despite the stress on the outpouring of the Spirit as the sign of Christ's exaltation (Acts 2:1ff.), has always been present in the history of God's people and did not first appear with Christ. In the course of Israel's history, the Jews have always resisted the Holy Spirit (Acts 7:51); they have persecuted the prophets rather than listening to them (7:52); the prophet Moses was disavowed (7:25,40) and repudiated by the fact that the Jews did not keep the law (7:53). Pentecost added nothing radically new to the history of God's people: through the outpouring of the Spirit Israel becomes the people of the Spirit (2:17–18); what we encounter in the Christian community, the sons of the prophets (3:25), is the portion of the people which does not resist the Spirit. Today this Spirit is present in the community, and there are also the prophets (2:17;

---

[111] Elsewhere Luke names the patriarchs.
[112] Only Luke within the New Testament calls David a prophet.

13:1ff.; 21:10 etc.). There are no prophets in the synagogue, which does not mean that the Spirit is not present; the Scriptures are read there (13:27), and for Christians the synagogue is the house of the Scriptures. When Christians appear in the synagogue and interpret the Scriptures, the Spirit is obviously also present, though many resist him. In the community the Spirit is present in the Scriptures as well as in the believers (4:25,31).

As the prophet, David is also the father of the Messiah and the king of Israel (Acts 13:22; Luke 1:32). As such he plays a great role in Luke's interpretation of Scriptures, and in a certain 'negative' respect as well. David himself is a witness to the fact that individual utterances of Scripture do not apply to David. This polemic-negative interpretation of Scripture used by Luke in this connection, and addressed to the synagogue, is unique to the New Testament. In Acts 2:14–35, Psalm 16:8–11 is cited in 2:25–8 and interpreted in 2:29–31. 'To this day', that is when Luke writes, David's tomb is to be found in Jerusalem (2:29), which indicates that David is not and was never meant to be the risen Messiah. David cannot be the subject, since he saw corruption, and the *topos* of Messiah's resurrection deals precisely with corruption, as this is what the Scripture says (2:27,31). Luke counters the notion that David is or will be the subject of this psalm. He does so with rational and illuminating arguments, not with esoteric mysteries of scriptural exposition: the Scripture applies only to Christ, and to this the prophet David is the first prophetic witness (2:30); he speaks not of himself, but of his son (2:30–1). David is the prophetic king whose posterity is, in the resurrection, portrayed as the Messiah of Israel, and the resurrection means the enthronement of the charismatic Messiah. But David did not ascend to heaven, as Luke emphasizes (2:34), and the text used (Ps. 110:1) does not deal with David at all, but with Jesus. For this reason it was not David who poured out the Spirit. The prophet *par excellence*, David, is here surpassed by his son. The hearers can see and hear for themselves that Israel's Messiah is presently active through the Spirit. What is at issue for Luke is set forth in the conclusion (2:36): Jesus is the charismatic Messiah of Israel, the true descendant of David, the prophet-king. Israel's traditions are in a unique way connected here with the charismatic experience of primitive Christianity. David is the central figure in the Scriptures and so in history. The authoritative words of David in Scripture contain the truth of the Christian proclamation.

Paul's first speech in Acts 13:16–41 contains a survey of Israel's history (13:17–25), but also no less than four scriptural quotations (13:33,34 and 35), which in itself is striking, since there are scarcely any scriptural quotations in Paul's speeches elsewhere in Acts.[113] Luke is content to state that everything Paul says agrees with Scripture (24:14; 26:22). Paul, whom Luke regards as a charismatic, chiefly appears as interpreter of Scripture. Historical survey (13:17–25) and kerygma (13:26–31) are so interwoven that the kerygma is understood as a link in the history of Israel. Israel's history is narrated in such a fashion that it is orientated to David as its culmination (v. 22); of David's posterity (v. 22), God has brought to Israel a saviour (v. 23); the contemporary hearers, the Israel of today, are given the sure promises or words of David (v. 34); and so we have the negative proof from Scripture (vv. 35–7): David saw corruption (v. 36). Luke's exposition of Psalm 16 in verses 35–7 is unintelligible taken in isolation, but clear with the aid of Acts 2:25ff. The author of Psalm 16 is God (cf. the preambles to the quotations in 13:32,34 and 36): David saw 'corruption' (v. 35) and, in addition, it is said that David served God 'in his own generation'. The clear historical dimension here in the exposition of the Scripture is that David no longer serves God as he once did. His significance now lies in his scriptural words,[114] in his promises which have already been fulfilled (13:37–9). The story of David and consequently of Israel is misunderstood when it is not interpreted as culminating in Jesus. This culmination can be demonstrated not only by quoting individual words

---

[113] Apart from Acts 13 only in Acts 28:25–8.
[114] The passage is to be understood in this sense if 'the holy and sure blessings of David' are to be construed as scriptural promises of David, a view strongly suggested by the context.

of Scripture, but also by means of historical survey combined with the kerygma.

In David the prophetic and messianic conjoin. As the prophetic element is united to Scripture, it is all but inconceivable that the Jews did not recognize Jesus and acknowledge him, as he actually is proclaimed through the reading of the prophets on the sabbath (Acts 13:27). The dwellers in Jerusalem and the leaders have not understood the utterances of the prophets (13:27), though these are continually read aloud. Luke does not appeal to a theory of hardening for an explanation, nor to an enlightened, charismatic reading of Scriptures. He argues in a 'rational' fashion: if one knows the Scriptures and David's history, one should clearly understand Jesus' messianic significance. That Jesus' true significance is proclaimed in the synagogue and through the recitation of Scriptures on the sabbath is also shown by the fact that some in Israel have understood the salvation in Jesus.

The negative-polemic use of Scripture in Acts 2 and 13, which reflects a discussion with the synagogue, indicates that the messiahship of Jesus and the salvation of Israel are at stake when Scriptures are not understood. The Scriptures in themselves are clear. Luke finds no mysteries in the wording, there is no 'spiritual' understanding, but only the literal. Nevertheless, Luke sometimes states that the Scriptures must be opened (Acts 17:3; Luke 24:32,45, cf. Acts 8:31, 35).[115] In Luke 24:25–7 the disciples do not understand the Scriptures until Jesus has interpreted them; the subject is that which is written of Jesus himself (v. 27): thus, Jesus 'opened' the Scriptures (cf. Luke 24:45). In Acts 8:31 the Ethiopian chamberlain cannot understand the Scriptures without instruction. The portion of the Scriptures to be explained in Acts 8:32–3 is Isaiah 53:7f., but in fact it is not interpreted by Philip, as an explanation is superfluous; the only important question is: 'About whom does the prophet say this, about himself or about someone else?' So

---

[115] On this concept: G. Delling, ' "... als er uns die Schrift aufschloss". Zur lukanischen Terminologie der Auslegung des Alten Testaments', in H. Balz and S. Schulz (eds.), *Das Wort und die Wörter: FS* G. Friedrich *zum 65. Geburtstag*, Stuttgart 1973, 75ff.

Luke can content himself with having Philip preach about Jesus, obviously with the help of the Scriptures (8:35). The chamberlain's question in 8:34 reflects the central theme of Luke's scriptural exposition, as is seen in Acts 2:25ff. and 13:34ff., where it is made clear that David did not write about himself. Only as one allows the Scripture in the relevant passages to speak of Jesus does an opening of Scripture occur; without, however, adding any new content. The only instruction needed is simply to apply the Scripture to Jesus. There is no hidden meaning in the Scriptures, as they speak clearly and unproblematically.[116] Acts is concerned not with suffering as such, for this is not offensive or alien to the Jews, but with the one to whom the sufferings actually happen, in the case in point the prophet himself or Jesus. Luke has no theory according to which Jesus himself must open the Scriptures if they are to be understood. Jesus is the first to interpret Scriptures with reference to himself, but this 'opening' is done subsequently by others, as is described in Acts, indirectly by the interpretation of Scripture – thus, for example, in the speeches in Acts 2 and 3 – directly, for example by Philip (8:35) or by Paul (17:3).

Next to David, Moses is an important witness to Jesus as Christ. He is obviously the lawgiver, but above all a prophet of Christ. Luke must demonstrate also that Moses has witnessed the story of Jesus. In Acts 3:22–3 and 7:37 we have an explanation of Deuteronomy 18:15–20, a portion of Scripture only to be found in Luke in the New Testament. All the prophets have the sufferings of the Messiah as their actual theme (Acts 3:18); all the prophets have proclaimed the days of Christ (3:24). God has spoken through the prophets 'from of old' (3:21). The prophetic is set forth as Israel's chief characteristic, and therefore the Jews are the sons of the prophets (3:25).[117] In this respect, Luke is original. Moses himself is a

---

[116] That an 'external' event opens the Scriptures is often the case with Luke. Acts 13:46–7: because the Jews now reject the gospel, the time for Scripture has come – it summons Israel, in this case the church, to go to the Gentiles (Isa. 49:6). Acts 15:15ff.: the experiences of the missionaries made clear how Scripture is to be understood; the Scripture is Amos 9:11f. The external events 'agree with' the Scripture.

[117] See further above, the section 'The people of the Spirit'.

prophet, who also preached beforehand Jesus as the coming
prophet (3:22); not only so, but Moses prophesied the fate of the
Jews who rejected Jesus: everyone who does not hearken to this
prophet will be destroyed from among the people (3:23). Moses
is plainly portrayed as a prophet, and as the prophet 'from of
old', so that all others take after him (3:18,21,22). The charismatic–prophetic quality in Moses is further detailed in Acts 7,
again with a quotation of Deuteronomy 18:15 in 7:37. Added
here is that Moses is portrayed as a miracle-worker (7:36); he
performed 'wonders and signs' in Egypt. Moses' performance
of miracles and his prophetic activity are also combined with
the giving of the law (7:38), so that Moses represents that very
combination of Spirit and law which is decisive for Luke's
description of the primitive community. In this respect the law
is subordinated to the charismatic, but still a part of it. The
preaching of the prophet Moses and the other prophets has
exactly the same content (Acts 26:22–3). Paul merely preached
what the prophets and Moses[118] predicted would come to pass
– the death and resurrection of the Messiah, and the mission.
The entire Christian message can be found in Moses, so that he
is to be understood as a witness to Christ.

For Luke, Moses is primarily a prophet and witness to Christ.
Since Moses was recited aloud in the synagogue, there was also
there a preaching of Christ. But he is the lawgiver as well. So
'the law' is a prophetic word, and it is a ritual and moral code.
The prophetic words of God are spoken 'from eternity', while
the law was added at a definite, later point in time (Acts
7:38,53). If the prophetic words are God's very own words, the
ipsissima vox, the law appears by the disposition of angels (7:53).

With the prophetic element at the centre of Scripture, the
notion of promise and fulfilment is important to Luke. His idea,
however, is not that the Scripture as a whole represents the
promises whereas the Jesus-event and the church give the
fulfilment. This is why Scripture contains far more than just
promises. The Scriptures are not just throughout an arsenal of

[118] 'The prophets and Moses' in this passage is not an expression for Scripture in
general. He is obviously thinking of specific passages in the various writings,
without citing them. The exception is Deut. 18:15–20.

the promises, which we can refer to and take as proof of God's power over history, and so also a guarantee for the future of the church. This aspect is there in Luke's thought, but there is more to it. The Scriptures tell us of both promises and fulfilments, contain both parts, and this even in the time before Messiah. The promises deal with all parts of the life of Israel, not only with the Messiah question. The whole history of Israel told in the Scriptures is the history of a succession and intermingling of promises and fulfilments.[119] God gave the people promises which he fulfilled at various times in the course of history, whereafter he gives new promises; he even fulfils portions of the promises at one time and the rest at another. In the Scriptures you have promises, fulfilments, new promises, a portion of promises fulfilled, and this goes on even in the time of the church. The time of the promises does not belong to the past for Luke; there are still promises which in the future shall be fulfilled, such as the parousia and the coming of the kingdom. This way of thinking is clearly demonstrated in the Stephen-speech as a whole (Acts 7; cf. vv. 3,5,6,7,17,23,37,52, see also Acts 1:4; 2:1,33,39; 13:23,32; Luke 1:20; 9:31,51; 21:24; 22:16; 24:44).

Scripture is Israel's Scripture. It belongs to Israel and is a word to Israel. This is so obvious to Luke that it is unnecessary to explain it. He gives it repeated expression. What Luke must set forth explicitly is that the church is Israel, and that the church precisely as Israel has title to the Scripture.

The history that Scripture describes is that of Israel; the history of the Gentile nations is not a history of God's acts and not a history of salvation. For this reason Scripture also does not furnish a history of the individual, but only of Israel, and a history of Gentiles in so far as they have a connection with Israel. This is clear from the historical résumés in Acts 7:2–53 and 13:17–25. Israel's history is introduced without any explanation, and precisely because it is Israel's history and consequently

---

[119] E. Lohse, 'Lukas als Theologe der Heilsgeschichte', *EvTh* 14, 1954, 254–75; P. Schubert, 'The Structure and Significance of Luke 24', in W. Eltester (ed.), *Neutestamentliche Studien für R. Bultmann zu seinem 70. Geburtstag*, BZNW 21, Berlin 1954, 165–85.

also the history of the church. The survey in 13:17–25 climaxes in the promise of a Saviour for Israel (v. 23). The Christian kerygma is a portion of this story, that is the story of how the word of salvation was, as it were, vigorously rejected by Jerusalem and thus also fulfilled (vv. 26–31). The Jews, in this case those in the Dispersion, are the children of salvation, heirs of the history of Israel; the words of Scripture thus apply to them. The entire speech (13:16–41) is addressed to Israelites (v. 16), and for Luke Israelites are Israelites in every sense of the term.

Sometimes the addressees of Scripture are designated 'the fathers'.[120] The Scripture was not written 'with reference to us', the Christians. The word of the impenitent people's hardening in Isaiah 6:1f. is applied by Paul to the unbelieving Jews at Rome (Acts 28:25–7): the word is spoken 'to the fathers' (v. 25). As God has spoken to the fathers, the Scripture is a word to Israel. Paul serves the 'God of our fathers' since he believes the Scriptures (24:14). God spoke directly to the fathers (7:3,37): God directs the history of Israel. And so the Jews are not only the sons of Israel, but especially 'the sons of the prophets' or 'of the covenant' (3:25): so they are the heirs of the prophets and of Scripture. But now the title to Scripture belongs to the true sons of the prophets, which means those who are endowed with the Spirit (2:17ff.). The outpouring of the Spirit on 'sons and daughters' (2:17) is not legitimized by the mere occurrence, but by the Scriptures, and only thus described as God's Spirit (2:16).

It is not only David, Moses and the prophets who belong to the centre of Scripture, but Israel as well. The issue is salvation for Israel, and thus also the rebuilding of the 'dwelling of David' (Acts 15:16), that is the Jewish-Christian community. Israel's claim to Scripture is self-evident because Israel is the people of God and thus also of the Scripture. What takes place in the Gentile mission (15:7–9,12) is now shown to be in accord with Scripture and only in this fashion also legitimized; because it is prophesied in Scripture that the salvation of Gentiles will be linked to the destiny of Israel, so too the Gentile mission is

---

[120] 'The fathers' are evaluated positively (3:13,25; 5:30; 7:12; 22:14; 26:6) as well as negatively (7:38,45,51–3; 15:10; 28:25).

proved to be the legitimate concern of the people of God. By interpreting the resurrection as enthronement on the seat of David, Israel's title to Scripture is given (Acts 2:30–1). The impenitent Jews fulfil the Scriptures by crucifying and burying Jesus (Acts 13:27–9). This is a unique interpretation of Scripture fulfilment within the New Testament.[121]

The place of Scripture is the synagogue, so that Scripture has its 'home' in the house of Israel. Scripture does not exist for private reading.[122] It belongs to recitation and exposition in the synagogal worship of God (9:20; 13:5,14,27; 14:1; 17:1–2,10f.,17; 18:4; 19:8,20).[123] We may not interpret these scenes in the synagogues as a tactical missionary pragmatism on the part of Paul. When Paul visits the synagogue in Thessalonica (17:1–4), the reason does not lie in his missionary activity, but in Jewish faith and Paul's piety, 'according to Paul's custom'. In 17:11 it is assumed that Israel's Scripture is involved. The church leads the Jews toward the Scripture: on the basis of Scripture, 'if these things were so' (17:11–12), the Jews come to faith.

The content of the centre of the Scriptures is found chiefly in the summaries (3:18; 10:43; 17:3; 18:28; 26:22–3; Luke 24:26,46); the subject is first of all the suffering and death of Messiah (3:18; 17:3; 26:22; Luke 24:26,46). The utterances are fairly consonant: the subject is not suffering in itself, the question is whether Scripture gives witness that it was the Messiah who had to suffer and die. The identity of the suffering one is important (Acts 8:34): the question is whether the prophet himself is the suffering one, thus whether the suffering already belongs to history. The 'someone else' (8:34) is the Messiah, a feature which is also stressed in 3:18; 17:3; 26:22,46. Witness to the towering significance of the Messiah's suffering death as furnishing content to the centre of Scripture appears also in 13:29: the Jews have fulfilled all that was written of Jesus; the 'all' in

---

[121] But cf. Rom. 13:8.

[122] The only exception is the Ethiopian chamberlain (Acts 8:22ff.).

[123] This is connected to the fact that Luke understands the words of the Scripture as spoken. In the New Testament, only Luke makes any mention of the reading of the Scriptures on the sabbath (Acts 13:27; 15:21; Luke 4:16, but cf. 2 Cor. 3:15).

this passage means simply suffering and death. Not only the summaries in general, but also individual passages, indicate suffering as the mark of the Messiah's identity (4:25; 5:30; 8:32).[124]

In the second place, the summaries deal with the resurrection, the exaltation of this very suffering Messiah. This is variously formulated (17:3; 26:22–3; Luke 24:26,46). The problem of witnessing to the resurrection as such is not the issue: Luke knows that Jews believe in it, or at least most Jews do (Acts 26:6ff.). The question at stake is: 'Who is the resurrected One?' Luke is concerned to show that it is not David but his descendant, the Messiah-Jesus (2:25ff.; 13:33ff.). The polemical account indicates that Luke is most intent on showing that the story of Jesus is in harmony with Scripture and that the Scripture applies only to Jesus: the Messiah witnessed to in Scripture can only be Jesus (3:18,21; 10:42,43; 17:3; 18:28; 26:22,23; Luke 24:16,27,44,46); with especial clarity it is stressed in Acts 3:18ff. and 13:33ff. that it is David's son and the king of Israel who must die and rise. What Jesus' death and resurrection really mean retreats for Luke behind the fact that they have to do with the son of David.

It is not only the history of Jesus, his death and resurrection, which are witnessed to in Scripture, but also other phenomena in the gospel and even in the history of the church: the death of Judas and the subsequent choice of an apostle (Acts 1:16f.,20ff.); the story of Pilate, the Romans and Herod (4:25ff.); the outpouring of the Spirit, the prophecies in the church and the miracles (Acts 2:17ff.); the parousia (Acts 3:21); the forgiveness of sins as the result of the death and resurrection of Jesus (Acts 10:43; Luke 24:26); the mission among Jews and Gentiles, starting in Jerusalem, and even the missionaries of the church (Luke 24:26,46f.; Acts 13:47; 15:15ff.; 26:22f.), the rejection of the gospel by parts of Israel (Acts 3:23; 13:41; 26:22; 28:26ff.); the whole gospel is read every sabbath in the synagogue as they read the Scriptures (Acts 13:27).

In the Scriptures you find the history of the former periods of

---

[124] No direct quotation, but the reference is clearly to Deut. 21:22 (LXX). 'The Christians' here are Luke and Paul (Acts 5:30; 10:39; Gal. 3:13).

Israel. But you also find the Jesus story and what happens in the church. There is no legitimacy for the church unless it can be displayed from Scripture.

THE TWELVE

'I appoint unto you the kingdom, which my father appointed unto me; you shall eat and drink at my table in my kingdom and sit on thrones judging the twelve tribes of Israel' (Luke 22:29–30). In the unique farewell discourse in Luke 22:24–30 the Twelve are given an eschatological role as the future regents over Israel.[125] The text signals Luke's conception of the apostolate.[126] In the question from the Twelve (Acts 1:6) the resurrection and the outpouring of the Spirit are interpreted as heralding the restoration of Israel. In Acts 1:15–26 we have the election of a new apostle – why is it necessary to elect a new, twelfth apostle? [127] Luke's conception of the twelve apostles is shaped by his theology of Israel, and the Twelve are essential to his understanding of Israel and its fate.

The significance of the Twelve is indicated by Luke's composition. The apostles play no role in the latter half of Acts, being mentioned for the last time in connection with the Apostolic Council (Acts 15:2,4,22f.; 16:4).[128] Their role shifts after chapter 7: Stephen's sermon marking the conclusion of the missionary activity in Jerusalem signifies the end of the apostles' direct missionary activity to Israel. The initial reference to the peoples outside Israel (Acts 10–11) is related to one of the Twelve, Peter – this reference to 'the nations' is part of the promise to Israel. Outside chapters 10–11, Acts records no missionary activity among the Gentiles by the Twelve. Acts 8:14ff. connects the

---

[125] The presupposition that Luke sees the church as an independent entity in distance from and break with Judaism, as a new Israel, has determined the understanding of the twelve apostles as the origin of ecclesiastical offices.

[126] Some scholars find the text as a vestige or reminiscence of Jewish-Christian tradition with no meaning for Luke's conception of the apostolate.

[127] Scholars find a contrast between this statement and the theology of Luke as a whole and therefore assign it to one or more pre-Lucan Jewish traditions. But why pick up a Jewish-Christian tradition if it was of no importance to Luke?

[128] The problem of the disappearance of the Twelve from the picture in Acts is 'one of the most distressing in Acts', Haenchen, *Acts*, 336.

Twelve with the mission in Samaria, which is not a Gentile
mission, since for Luke the Samaritans are considered not to be
Gentiles, but 'the lost sheep of the house of Israel'.[129] The
Twelve are also connected with Paul (9:26ff.), who is a Dispersion missionary and teacher of Israel. The problem dealt with
in Acts 15 is the relationship of the Gentiles to the law of Moses,
and the apostles disappear from the narrative at this point
because their mission to Israel is accomplished.

During Jesus' earthly life the apostles play a notably passive
role. They participate mainly as observers of the events, as do
the other disciples and even the entire Jewish population. For
Luke, the life of Jesus is not enveloped in secrecy, as everything
happens in public, while all Israel watches;[130] the Twelve's task
is not to be eyewitnesses, to guarantee the Jesus-tradition, as
this tradition is well known to all Jews (Acts 2:22; 10:37f.).
Sayings of Jesus are therefore seldom found on the lips of the
apostles in Acts.

They play a more determinative role on two occasions. The
first occurs in the account of the Lord's Supper (Luke 22:14ff.),
in the part of the passion story Luke most thoroughly reworked
(22:24–37), that is Jesus' farewell discourse.[131] Luke 24:28–30 is
Jesus' last will and testament:[132] here the future role of the
Twelve is decisive, since they will excercise authority just as
Jesus has done;[133] the Twelve are not ecclesiastical regents, but
regarded as Israel's eschatological rulers and judges. [134]

Luke shows great concern for the events occurring between

---

[129] J. Jervell, *People of God*, 113–32.

[130] Cf. passages like 3:7,10,21; 4:14f.,23,37,44; 5:17; 7:1,3,17; 8:4,40; 11:29; 12:1,54; 13:22;
14:25; 15:1f.; 16:14; 18:18,36,43; 19:7,47,48; chapters 20–4 *passim*.

[131] The material derives from Mark (10:41ff.), from Q (Luke 22:30 = Matt. 19:28) and
finally from Luke's special material (22:28–9). As a composition, the discourse is
undoubtedly Luke's work.

[132] Within the framework of a farewell discourse *diathēkē* means 'last will and
testament'; cf. R. Bultmann, *History of the Synoptic Tradition*, Oxford 1963, 159;
H. Schürmann, *Eine quellenkritische Untersuchung des lukanischen Abendmahlberichtes* III,
Jesu Abschiedsrede, Münster 1956, 41f.

[133] R. Bultmann, *Theology of the New Testament*, New York 1955, I, 17; H. von
Campenhausen, *Ecclesiastical Authority and Spiritual Power*, London 1969, 16; W.G.
Kümmel, *Promise and Fulfilment*, Napierville 1957, 47.

[134] The very location in the composition makes it unlikely that Luke in this important
discourse is simply handing on Jewish-Christian reminiscenses without their having
any meaning for him.

Jesus' death and the outpouring of the Spirit (Luke 24 and Acts 1): the Twelve are especially associated with the resurrection, and this is to be expected in light of the definitive statement in Acts 1:21. It is generally accepted that the Twelve function as guarantors of the ecclesiastical tradition, i.e. of the normative Jesus-tradition that they can confirm in detail.[135] This is not correct. The witness of the apostles does not concern Jesus' life; the speeches in Acts very seldom allude to the life of Jesus apart from referring to the murder of the Messiah (2:23,36; 3:14; 4:10,27f.; 5:28 etc.), and when we find a reference to the earthly Jesus, it is expressly stated that the listeners themselves are acquainted with what has happened, so that the apostles need not tell about it (2:22).[136] The fullest reference to the life of Jesus occurs in 10:38, but even here the listeners themselves are said also to be aware of everything that happened and that Jesus had said (10:37, cf. Luke 24:19). Any such guarantee is therefore superfluous, and this has to do with the public character of of Jesus' entire ministry according to Luke;[137] the entire life of Jesus, and his words, are so widely known that it is not necessary for the Twelve to be guarantors of them. In the speeches, the only thing the listeners do not seem to know about is Jesus' resurrection (2:24ff.,32; 3:15). In Acts 1:21f. the qualification for the new apostle is the requirement that he has been with the eleven between the baptism of John and the ascension of Jesus, not his resurrection. This is because of the forty days when Jesus gave his important instruction about his resurrection as the hope of Israel. There were more witnesses to the resurrection than the apostles, but they alone knew Jesus'

---

[135] H. Conzelmann, *Theology of St Luke*, 216; E. Haenchen, *Acts*, 163, 353; E. Hennecke and W. Schneemelcher (eds.), *New Testament Apocrypha*, Philadelphia 1964, II, 29f.; E. Schweizer, *Church Order in the New Testament*, London 1961, 69f.

[136] The Western text has found this so remarkable that it makes an alteration, so that it turns out to be apostles who know about the miracles and become witnesses.

[137] Even though Luke does not stress the apostles' special knowledge of Jesus and his message in Acts, it is conceivable that it is not necessary to re-emphasize what is said in the Gospel. But even in the Gospel the apostles do not know more than others; there is nothing like an esoteric instruction (cf. Mark 4:10ff. and Luke 8:4ff.; Mark 9:35ff. and Luke 9:46; Mark 8:14ff. and Luke 12:1ff.; Mark 9:28 and Luke 9:43; Mark 10:2ff. and Luke 16:1ff.,14; Mark 10:17ff. and Luke 18:24; Mark 12:41ff. and Luke 21:1ff.; Mark 13:1,2,3,23 and Luke 21:5,7).

teaching about the true meaning of this event. Therefore the
instruction is clear: they shall be witnesses to the resurrection.
This is repeatedly made very clear. The announcement of the
discovery of the empty tomb was given to 'the eleven and all the
rest' (Luke 24:9). The travellers to Emmaus are to take to the
eleven the news that their doubt about Jesus as Israel's
redeemer has been dispelled (24:21,25ff.,33f.) – once among the
apostles they find that they already believe (24:34). The leader
of the Twelve is the first to have received a christophany
(24:34). The resurrection speech in 24:36–49 was primarily
directed to the eleven (24:9f.,33f.; Acts 1:2f.). It is to the Twelve
Jesus reveals himself after his resurrection (Acts 1:3, cf. 13:31;
10:41). In the third passion/resurrection prediction the Twelve
are again set apart (Luke 18:31–4). They are set apart wherever
the resurrection, the Messiah of Israel, or the redemption of
God's people are discussed. The opening chapter of Acts is
devoted entirely to Jesus' last meeting with the eleven apostles
(1:1–14) and to the story of the election of a new apostle (1:15–
26). In the prelude to Acts (1:1–14), we have an interpretation of
what Luke has said in his Gospel (vv. 2–4,12–14), a dialogue
between Jesus and the eleven (vv. 6–8), and a short account of
the ascension (vv. 9–11). In the period following the resurrection
Jesus spent forty days teaching the eleven about the kingdom of
God (1:3). Luke relates the preaching of the eleven directly to
Jesus' preaching and the line is also drawn back to the farewell
discourse (Luke 22:24ff.), especially to the saying that the
Twelve shall be entrusted with *basileia* in the same way Jesus
received it (22:29).[138] This *basileia* is linked to the restoration of
Israel, it is 'the kingdom of Israel' (22:29f.). Luke connects
messiahship with the kingdom of God (Luke 1–2; 24:21ff.,44ff.;
Acts 1:3,6); in light of the resurrection there is no longer any
doubt that the kingdom will be restored to Israel, and reference
is made to such a restoration, primarily in Acts 15:16ff. Two
things are clear: first, the task of the Twelve is to bear witness to
the resurrection of Jesus (1:22);[139] secondly, there must be

---

[138]   *Basileia* here means 'reign' and not 'realm'.
[139]   Acts 1:21f. does not say that the apostles are to be witnesses to Jesus' earthly life;
their witness is tied exclusively to the resurrection.

twelve apostles, at least during a certain period of history (1:15–26) – after the death of James (Acts 12:2) it would be superfluous to elect a new apostle.

Why does Luke have to inform us about the election of a twelfth apostle, describing the election as the fulfilment of Scripture and as an election by God himself?[140] The link between the number twelve and the apostolic circle is traditional, but Luke reveals that the precise number twelve as applied to the apostolic circle is essential, and that this circle can only function with the correct number. In the account of Judas' betrayal, Luke is not satisfied with the description of Judas as 'one of the Twelve',[141] but uses the elaborate description of Judas 'of the number of the Twelve' (Luke 22:3). Judas belongs to a group for which the number twelve is constitutive. We have the same emphasis in Acts 1:17, 'he was numbered among us, and was allotted his share in this ministry'; and in Acts 1:26, Matthias was 'enrolled[142] with the eleven apostles'. The number twelve is important because the circle of the Twelve is linked explicitly to the concept 'Israel' (Luke 22:30).[143] In Acts 26:6f. the fulfilment of the promise of the resurrection is the focal point of Israel's worship, and in this connection Israel is the people of the twelve tribes. Luke links Israel–*basileia*– resurrection–messiahship.

The Twelve will serve as regents in the eschatological Israel (Luke 22:30);[144] in the account in Acts 1:21f., the task of the

---

[140] There is a widespread uncertainty about the meaning of Acts 1:15–26; it has to do with 'the sacred number twelve', H. Conzelmann, *Acts of the Apostles*, Hermeneia, Philadelphia 1987, 12; E. Haenchen, *Acts*, 164; P.-H. Menoud, 'Les additions au groupe des douzes apôtres d'après le livre des Actes', *RHPhR* 37, 1957, 71–80; the apostolic circle must have the same modus as it had during the life of Jesus, G. Klein, *Die zwölf Apostel*, FRLANT 77, Göttingen 1961, 206; the link between the former time of Jesus and the missionary church must be clear, G. Schneider, *Die Apostelgeschichte* I, HThK V/1, Freiburg/Basle/Vienna 1980, 213; the circle must be complete etc.

[141] So Mark 14:10; Matt. 26:14.

[142] The numerical significance for this infrequent verb in classical Greek is indicated by the parallels Luke 22:3, Acts 1:17, and Acts 19:19.

[143] Luke's statement differs from Matt. 19:28 in lacking the number twelve with regard to the thrones, as he gives careful consideration to Judas. He is present at the farewell discourse and so Luke cannot let Jesus give the Twelve the promise of being judges over Israel.

[144] There is some diagreement whether *krinein* here means 'to judge' or 'to rule'. For

Twelve consists in bearing witness to Jesus' resurrection. What is the connection between these two statements?[145] According to Luke, resurrection-faith is a real concern for Israel, 'God's promise to the fathers' and 'Israel's hope' (Acts 26:6ff.), and the resurrection is characterized as a specifically pharisaic faith (Acts 26:5; 23:6–8); resurrection is the fulfilment of Scripture (26:22–3; Luke 24:25–7,32,44–6). In his Gospel Luke is content with general references to Moses in dealing with what Scripture says about the resurrection, whereas in Acts he gives detailed exegesis on this point (2:25ff.; 13:23ff.). Here he links the Davidic messianic concept of the *basileia* to the resurrection (2:30; 13:33f.). Since the primary task of the Twelve, according to Acts 1:22, is to witness to the resurrection, the connection with the farewell discourse concerning the twelve regents over the twelve tribes of Israel is clear (Luke 22:30). The *basileia* Jesus proclaims is the kingdom Israel waits for, which has been promised to the people of God (Acts 1:3,6; Luke 1:32,33). God will give Jesus the throne of his father David;[146] his kingdom will be without end.[147] The agreement with Acts 2:30 is obvious: God has sworn to set 'one of David's descendants upon his throne'. Within this concept of the resurrection as enthronement (Acts 2:29–32) the Twelve are included as witnesses (2:32b). David himself had spoken of the resurrection of the Messiah as fulfilling the promise to Israel (2:31); the Twelve may now proclaim Jesus as Lord and Messiah before 'the whole house of Israel' (2:36). The testimony of the Twelve

the first opinion, see G. Schrenk, *Die Weissagung über Israel im Neuen Testament*, 1951, 17ff.; K.H. Rengstorf, *TDNT* II, 327; for the other view: R. Bultmann, *Theology of the New Testament* I, 37; W.G. Kümmel, *Promise and Fulfilment*, 47; E. Stauffer, *New Testament Theology*, 1961, 308.

145 As no direct connection is immediately apparent, commentators maintain that the eschatological function of the Twelve according to Luke 22 disappears because of the historicizing tendency in Acts, so Haenchen, *Acts*, 164; or it continues to live on only as a weak traditional reminiscence, B. Lindars, *New Testament Apologetic*, London 1961, 187.

146 H. Conzelmann, *Theology of St Luke*, 166, claims that the Old Testament figures play no role in Luke's historical schema. For another view, cf. N.A. Dahl, 'The Story of Abraham in Luke–Acts', 139.

147 Concerning the understanding of Jesus as a Jewish king, see H. Cadbury, *The Making of Luke–Acts*, New York 1927, 277f. Cadbury maintains that Luke more than any other New Testament writer brings the current messianic hope of Judaism, but that Luke 'can scarcely have ever held this political view of the matter himself…'

is that God has fulfilled his promise to his people. The Spirit also testifies that Israel's Messiah has come (2:33ff.).

In Luke's Gospel, the whole of the first two chapters is permeated with the thought that the inauguration of the last phase of history, beginning with Jesus, is nothing but the fulfilment of God's promise to the fathers (1:16–17,32–3,51–4, 68–79; 2:10–11,25,29–32,38). We have the same theme about resurrection and Israel's salvation in the speeches in Acts 3:11ff.,18–22; 5:30; 10:42; 13:16ff.,23,31ff.; 15:16–18. The Twelve function as missionaries to the Jews;[148] they are called to proclaim before Israel that the turning-point in the history of the people of God has occurred and thereby to call the people to repentance for their putting Messiah to death. Luke assigns them a prophetic role (Acts 2:22f.,36,39; 3:13ff.,19ff.,24ff.; 4:10ff.,27; 5:30ff.).

The office of the Twelve as regents and judges is further illuminated by the division Luke recognizes between the people of Israel and their leaders. There is no salvation for all Israel (Acts 3:23). While the leaders reject the proclamation of the Messiah-Jesus, large segments of the people accept it; in scene after scene in Acts the Jewish leaders are portrayed as obdurate. The division in the people illustrates that Israel as a people is not rejected along with her leaders. The leaders of the people have relinquished any right to rule over the people, and the Twelve have now become the new leaders of Israel, as Luke 22:30 makes clear. They are therefore presented in Acts both as leaders and as those who proclaim the fulfilment of the promise to the people. They rule not over a special synagogue, a new organization or congregation, but simply over Israel. As Jesus addressed the people as a whole and made demands on them, so do his successors, the Twelve.

Luke's concern for the Twelve is not for an office, in the sense that such a college of twelve will always be found within the church to guide it; the Twelve are not the first ecclesiastical officials.[149] They are a singular phenomenon, as is clear from the eschatological emphasis of Luke 22:30: these chosen ones

---

[148] E. Haenchen, *Acts*, 144, n.1; the Twelve are relatively insignificant as missionaries.
[149] The idea that Luke represents 'early Catholicism' is clearly wrong as is seen from

will rule over Israel in the last times, which have come. Luke
does not trace ecclesiastical offices back to the Twelve; they do
not institute offices, transfer authority and install office-holders.
There are no permanent institutions and offices in the church.
This is because the church is the continuation, with new regents
and judges, of Israel's history at the end time.

PAUL – THE TEACHER OF ISRAEL

Acts is, to a great extent, a book on Paul. To him alone
seventeen chapters, Acts 9 and 13 to 28, are devoted. Above all,
it is Paul whom Luke sets out to describe. He carries no title in
Acts: in passing, Luke can name him an 'apostle' (Acts 14:4,14),
but it is not necessary for Luke to use any title in order to show
his position in the church. Luke knows about the Twelve and
even about other apostles. It seems a paradox that the title
'apostle' is not used in connection with Paul, in spite of the fact
that he is the only world missionary and 'ecumenical'
missionary, the leader of the church. But, to Luke, Paul is
something more than can be expressed by the means of this
title. No one compares to him, not even the Twelve. The
Twelve are important as a group, whereas Paul stands out as an
individual. Very little information is given about the Twelve,
and almost none about the leader and authority in the
Jerusalem church, James, the brother of the Lord,[150] but Luke
fills up Acts with information on Paul, as if he were an
unknown. Yet Paul is, to the readers of Acts, the most well-
known figure in the church, so Luke repeats what his readers
already know. The intention is obviously not to tell the story of
Paul, but to explain and defend him and his role, as he is a
most controversial figure, in the church as well as for the Jewish
world. If the church is the true Israel, what about Paul's
statements about Israel and the law? Does the greatest part of
the church stem from a Jewish apostate?

Paul's unique position in the church is expressed through

his idea of the Twelve, his ecclesiology (not the new Israel) and from the
interpretation of the Scriptures (not the book written for the church).
[150]   Acts 12:17; 15:13ff.; 21:18ff.

the three reports of his conversion and vocation, Acts 9, 22 and 26. A biographical conversion story such as this is given only in connection with Paul. The first of the three reports we find at the beginning of the mission to the Dispersion, initiated by Paul in Damascus, and combined with the mission to the Gentiles, that is the God-fearers (Acts 9:19ff.); the other two, Acts 22 and 26, we find in the apologetic speeches in Paul's trial (Acts 21–8).[151]

In the reports about the conversion Luke has made use of a pattern

(1.) A description of Paul's life as an orthodox Jew, his education and training in Jerusalem and his pharisaism (22:3; 26:4–5).

(2.) Paul as persecutor of the Christian churches (9:1–2; 22:4–5; 26:9–11); Paul cites leading Jews as witnesses (9:13; 22:5; 26:5).

(3.) The Damascus vision (9:3–7; 22:5–16; 26:12–18).

(4.) Paul's missionary commision, formulated quite differently in the three accounts (9:15; 22:17–21; 26:16b–18).[152]

Paul's unique position in the church is clear. He did not come as a missionary from a church or from an apostolic tradition, but was commissioned directly by God himself. What Paul experienced at Damascus is comparable only to the situation of the Twelve: there is a christophany, the Lord reveals himself to Paul and Paul sees Jesus (9:3–5,27; 22:6ff.,14; 26:19). Only the Twelve and Paul have seen Jesus as the risen Lord, and this fact establishes the apostolate; the connection between seeing Jesus and functioning as an apostle is made by Luke (Acts 1:21f.). Paul has the apostolic qualifications, being able to testify to the resurrection of Jesus (Acts 1:22b), which is decisive for the kerygma (Acts 2:23ff.,32; 3:15; 4:2,10,33; 5:32;

---

[151] There are considerable differences between the three accounts. The differences cannot be explained as the result of the use of written sources or by appealing to Luke's intention in each case individually, so E. Haenchen, *Acts*, 325ff.; Luke obviously had before him various traditions regarding the story of Paul's conversion.

[152] This pattern can be traced back to Paul's defence of his missionary activity and his apostleship in the face of Jews and Judaizers (Phil. 3:3ff.; Gal. 1:13ff.; cf. also 1 Cor. 15:8f. and 2 Cor. 11:22).

13:33ff.; 17:31; 23:6,8; 26:6). Paul is chosen by God himself
(9:15; 22:14; 26:16), and so were the Twelve (Luke 5:1–11;
6:12–16), but no one else in the church. Even more important
are the words of the risen Lord to Paul. Through these words
Paul is distinguished from the Twelve – to no one else in the
church are such words given. Acts 22:14 states that the God of
the fathers had chosen Paul to hear the voice of the Righteous;
this is an extraordinary event: through these words Paul
becomes the first and only witness to the world, the 'ecumenical' apostle and missionary. The witness 'to the ends of the
earth' is the apostolic commission (Acts 1:8, cf. Luke 24:47); it
is to be a witness before Jews and Gentiles, Israel and the
nations, including even the geographical perspective, from
Jerusalem to 'the ends of the earth' (Acts 1:8, cf. Luke 24:47).
The only one who carries out the geographical vision of the
missionary and apostolic commission is Paul; this is told not
only in the report on his work (Acts 13–21), but in the words of
the risen Lord (9:15; 22:15,17; 26:17–18) and in some summaries
(17:6; 20:21; 26:20).

The missionary commission is formulated with great varia-
tions. The three reports on the vocation of Paul are from
different traditions and reflect various ideas and thoughts about
the missionary work, above all the relation between Jews and
Gentiles as addressees for the preaching. It is, however, clear
that Luke consequently depicts Paul as the missionary to the
Jews. The place for the missionary work is above all the
synagogues, and this work starts immediately after Paul's conversion in the synagogues in Damascus (9:19f.,27); after that he
preached and debated with the Greek-speaking Jews in Jerusalem (9:28f.). From the church in Antioch Paul again visits the
synagogues in the Dispersion on his first missionary journey
(13:4,14,42f.; 14:1). After the Apostolic Council the missionary
efforts continue in the synagogues up until Paul's imprisonment
and trial (16:12f.; 17:1ff.,10f.,17; 18:4,19; 19:8). Paul never leaves
the synagogues and the Jews in order to go to the Gentiles.[153] A
great number of Jews are converted in all the synagogues, while

---

[153] In Acts 18:6 he leaves the synagogue in Corinth, but he continues his mission
before God-fearers and Jews in the same city, 18:7.

others reject the gospel; when the audience does not accept the gospel, the consequence is usually taken to be that Paul goes on to preach the gospel to Gentiles. And so Paul's Gentile mission appears, above all, to be the result of Jewish disobedience (13:46; 18:6).[154] This is obviously not correct: the Gentile mission is justified by reference to Scripture, not by Jewish disobedience (13:47); and despite the declaration of the missionaries in 13:46 and 18:6 Luke goes on to describe the Pauline mission in the synagogues (14:1; 16:12f.; 17:1,10,17; 18:4,19,26; 19:8) and the Pauline mission ends up with the Jews in Rome (28:17ff.). Paul does preach to Gentiles, but these Gentiles are the God-fearers, whom Paul meets in the synagogues, where he first addresses the Jews. When the repentant Jews are gathered and the unrepentant ones are excluded from the people of God, Paul turns also to the Gentiles.[155] When Gentiles are converted, it did not happen to the exclusion of the Jews, but in addition to them.[156] We find nowhere in Acts Paul addressing audiences which consist of Gentiles only.[157]

Paul is a missionary first to Jews, and only in addition to that and combined with this mission does he turn to Gentiles.[158] Luke's reason for stressing this point is clear in the apologetic speeches in Acts 21–8.[159] The entire section is devoted to Paul's

---

[154] So the great majority of the interpreters; otherwise: R.L. Brawley, *Luke–Acts and the Jews. Conflict, Apology, and the Conciliation*, SBLMS 3, Cambridge 1966, 69ff.; P. Esler, *Community and Gospel in Luke–Acts*, Cambridge 1978, 40f.; J. Jervell, *People of God*, 60ff.; M. Klinghardt, *Gesetz und Volk Gottes*, WUNT 32, Tübingen 1988, 237; B.J. Koet, *Five Studies on Interpretation of Scripture in Luke–Acts*, 106–18.

[155] P. Esler, *Community and Gospel*, 40f.: that Paul turns to the Gentiles 'means ... the deliberately public establishment of table-fellowship between Jews and Gentiles'.

[156] P. Esler, *Community and Gospel*, 39.

[157] Acts 14:18–14 is not a sermon and 17:22–31 is a polemical speech, not a missionary sermon, even if both speeches are addressed to Gentiles. This is clear not only with regard to form but also to content, that is, we miss in the Areopagus speech the most important elements, and where we have missionary preaching we always find mentioned the many conversions which took place.

[158] It is not correct to say that Luke has made the apostle to the Gentiles into a missionary to the Jews, nor to see this as a falsification of the historical Paul. Paul saw himself, primarily and in hindsight, as a missionary to the Jews; see 1 Cor. 9:20; Rom. 11:14,17ff.,25ff., and all the Jewish names among his companions and assistants, cf. Rom. 16; see J. Munck, *Paul and the Salvation of Mankind*, Richmond 1960, 36ff., 247ff.; *Christ and Israel. An Interpretation of Romans 9–11*, Philadelphia 1967, 116ff.

[159] The apologetic speeches of Paul have received only second-rate treatment com-

defence at his trial: that is, the addressees are the Jews, not the Romans. Luke grants as much space to Paul's trial as to his whole missionary activity, almost 50 per cent of his material on Paul.[160] His description of Paul in Acts is intended as a defence for the apostle. It is not necessary to describe Paul's missionary activity, but to explain and defend it. Luke's views are expressed, above all, in the choice and arrangements of material in the speeches. The speeches are of a strict biographical character and so what is said in the speeches is appropriate to Paul alone; he is not here serving as an example. According to common opinion the speeches represent political apologetic and are addressed to Rome, but this is out of the question, it is not political apologetic, but religious.

The prelude to the trial chapters and to the conclusion of Acts is a controversy concerning Paul's relationship to the law. Paul has taken leave of the churches he had founded, and has left behind for them his testament (Acts 20:17ff.). Paul is now, according to Luke, a well-known figure among Jews throughout the world. Rumours concerning his teaching and preaching have reached the Jews in Jerusalem (21:20ff.), and this leads to unrest among the tens of thousands of Christian Jews in Jerusalem who are zealous for the law; the problems are solved by Paul's demonstration of his fidelity to the law (21:20ff.). From 21:27 to the end of Acts, attention is focused on Paul and the Jews. The trial is never decided and leads not to Caesar, but to the Jews in Rome (28:17ff.); Paul has two meetings with them there. Here the final confrontation with the obdurate portion of Israel takes place. The trial is something more than a literary device to show how Paul reaches Rome and preaches in the world capital; the long drawn-out trial provides a broad framework, which makes it possible to accommodate four speeches by Paul, by means of which Luke can complete his description of the apostle.

The speeches are apologetic speeches, something Luke em-

---

pared to speeches in Acts 1–17. Yet the apologetic speeches represent more than 50 per cent of Paul's speeches in Acts.

[160] M. Dibelius, *Studies in the Acts of the Apostles*, London 1956, 149 finds the reason for this in Luke's wanting to aid and support persecuted Christians.

phasizes by using the words *apologeisthai* and *apologia* as catch-words (22:1; 24:10; 25:8; 26:1,2,24; 28:16). The intention of the speeches is not to carry on missionary work: there is no kerygma here,[161] no calls to repentance or conversion, no scriptural proof, no appeal to eyewitnesses. The object of defence in the speeches is not Christianity or the individual Christian, but the person and activity of Paul. In chapters 22 and 26 Luke makes use of preformed material,[162] and he comments on this material in chapters 23 and 24. Three factors in the speeches achieve decisive significance:

(1.) Paul was and is a Pharisee and a Jew who is faithful to the law (22:3; 23:1,3,5,6; 24:14; 26:4–5).

(2.) He believes everything that is written in the law and the prophets, and he teaches only what Scripture says; nothing in his preaching and teaching is un-Jewish (24:14f.; 26:22f.).

(3.) Paul is charged because he preaches the resurrection, but the resurrection expresses God's promises to the people and the hope of the pharisaic Israel (23:6; 24:21; 26:6–8); belief in the resurrection means fidelity to Scripture, law and people (24:14ff.; 26:22f.).

These elements reveal that Luke is concerned about the disquieting rumors concerning Paul occasioned by Jewish accusations (21:21).

Luke summarizes on several occasions the charges directed against Paul:

21:21: Paul teaches the Jews everywhere in the Dispersion apostasy from Moses, that they should not circumcise their children and that they do not need to live according to the customs of the fathers, the law.[163]

21:28: Paul teaches everywhere against the people, the law and the temple.

25:8: Paul has sinned neither against the law, the temple, nor Ceasar.

---

[161] It appears to be present in one passage, 26:23, but there it is not intended as preaching or proclamation, but as an apology for the content of Paul's preaching of Christ.

[162] J. Jervell, *People of God*, 163ff.

[163] The designation 'customs of the fathers' means the law, which is expressly stated in 6:13–14.

24:5f.: Paul had tried to profane the temple.

23:29: The Roman version of the Jewish charges is that the
problem concerns 'their [the Jews'] law' (cf. 25:19).

According to the charges Paul is a false teacher in Israel. At
issue is his teaching on the law and Israel, which concerns Jews
throughout the world. The charges do not relate to the mission
among the Gentiles,[164] and it does not emerge from the charges
that Paul is guilty of political rebellion.[165] The problem is
neither Paul's personal political innocence nor that of the
church in general.[166] But Paul has sinned against the people,
Israel (21:28; 28:17): he is charged with apostasy; he is guilty of
forsaking the law and is therefore no longer a member of the
people of God. At stake here is the justification of the church's
existence, and along with it the salvation of the Gentiles. The
controversy has to do with Paul's preaching.

Luke gives us only one missionary sermon of Paul (13:16–41);
his intention is to show the way Paul always preached in the
mission in the synagogues. The sermon is given to Jews on the
sabbath, but is applied also to Gentiles, namely the God-
fearers.[167] The sermon, addressed to the 'men of Israel' (13:16),
starts with a representation of the history of Israel (13:17–25), a
history determined by the faithfulness of God. The Jesus-event
is the summit of this history, and the promises to David are now
fulfilled for the people in the Dispersion (13:26ff.,32ff.). This
history has never been severed nor come to an end, in spite of
the opposition from the leaders and the people of Jerusalem,
who did not understand the Scriptures with their report of the
Christ-event (13:27ff.). The story continues without break in the
church. The fulfilment came through the resurrection, by which
Jesus was made the king of Israel (13:32ff.), and salvation, the
forgiveness of sins, is given through Jesus (13:38), not through
the law (13:39). This forgiveness is also justification, understood

---

[164] Against E. Haenchen, *Acts*, 100: the justification of the Gentile mission is the real
point of the speeches.
[165] Cf. J. Jervell, *People of God*, 166f.
[166] Ibid.
[167] It is a misunderstanding to see the sermon in Acts 13 as the type of sermons given
by Paul to Jews, whereas we find the type of sermons to Gentiles in the Areopagus
speech, 17:22–33.

as the aquittal of sins. Justification is given through faith, that is
through turning to the Messiah-king, not through the law of
Moses (13:39). To stick to the law does not give salvation,[168]
even if obedience to the law is necessary. The law has another
task.[169] The Jewish audience did not oppose the interpretation
of the law (13:42–3), but they contradicted Paul when, on the
following sabbath, they saw the crowds gathered to hear the
word of God and were filled with jealousy. There is, according
to Luke, no reason for the Jews to criticize Paul for his words on
the law. The sermon in 13:16–41 gives no clue to the charges
against Paul.

In Acts 20:18–35 we have Paul's farewell address to the
church, the only extant speech of his to the church. The speech
mentions in passing the content of Paul's proclamation: 'repentance before God and trust in our Lord Jesus' (20:21), the gospel
of God's grace (20:24) and 'proclaiming the kingdom' (20:25);
nothing is said about the law. The Jews are mentioned only
briefly with reference to their machinations (20:19). Not even
here does Luke mention anything to justify the harsh accusations from the Jews, accusations which he knows to be false.
Luke shows that it is impossible for Paul to have taught what he
is charged with having taught, but that, on the contrary Paul is
especially suited to be Israel's teacher. For Paul is a Pharisee,
faithful to the law and to Scripture, and thereby also true to
'the hope of Israel', the resurrection. Luke indicates in some
detail that Paul was born a Jew, raised in Jerusalem, faithful to
the law, a persecutor of Christian congregations (Acts 22:3–5;
24:4–5,9–11): this is not meant to serve as a demonstration of
the special mercy shown to the persecutor and Pharisee at
Damascus, for Paul is still a Pharisee and still faithful to the law
(23:6; 24:14–16); he is more faithful to the law than is the High
Priest (23:1ff.).[170] The description of the events leading to the

---

[168] This has nothing to do with the Pauline idea that the law as such cannot be
fulfilled, P. Vielhauer, 'The "Paulinism" of the Acts of the Apostles', in L.E. Keck
and J.L. Martyn (eds.), *Studies in Luke–Acts. Essays Presented in Honor of P. Schubert*,
Philadelphia ² 1980, 33ff.; correct: M. Klinghardt, *Gesetz und Volk Gottes*, 97ff.

[169] Forgiveness of sins is in Judaism not given through law-obedience, M. Klinghardt,
Gesetz und Volk Gottes, 101f.

[170] Cf. the charges against Stephen in 6:13–14 (he speaks against the holy place and the

Jewish plot against Paul in 24:17–24 says the same thing. Paul had come to Jerusalem to fulfil the supreme obligation of the law, almsgiving.[171] Luke notes in 24:17 that the alms are intended for the people,[172] yet Paul is charged with speaking against the people! But Paul sees himself as a member of the people and expresses through the alms his love for Israel. He is seized while fulfilling an obligation enjoined by the law, an offering in the temple (24:18). Thus whatever Paul was as a Pharisee, he still is as a Christian, except that he is no longer a persecutor.

Luke has more to say, and this is shown by another constantly recurring theme in the speeches, the resurrection. The resurrection is the very centre of the gospel. Belief in the resurrection is characterized as a pharisaic concern (Acts 23:1ff.) – as a Pharisee Paul must believe in the resurrection, 'the hope of Israel' (Acts 28:20).[173] In 26:6, where the catchword 'promise' appears, the resurrection expresses the promise made to the fathers. This promise, made to the fathers and the concern of the Pharisees, is also a concern of all twelve tribes of the people (26:7). To attain this is the goal of Jewish worship and practice (26:7); belief in the resurrection is the very heart of Jewish worship and the distinguishing mark of Israel. Here Luke substantiates the belief by reference neither to Jesus' resurrection nor to the eyewitness testimony of the Twelve: he proceeds from Scripture, the promises made to the fathers, pharisaism and the cult of the people. The polemical orientation is clear: Paul believes everything that the law and the prophets have said (Acts 24:14); what he preaches at no point goes beyond what Moses and the prophets have said about the Messiah and the future of the people, (26:22f.). Luke has Paul assert on several occasions that, in the final analysis, he is on trial because

---

law) and the last word in Stephen's speech in which he charges that the Jews have not kept the law (7:53). In the conflict between church and synagogue, the question as to who now keeps the law played a decisive role in the struggle for the right of membership in Israel.

[171] Cf. Luke 11:41; 12:33; Acts 9:36; 10:2,31.

[172] This is the Lucan interpretation of the collection of Paul.

[173] K. Haacker, 'Das Bekenntnis des Paulus zur Hoffnung Israels nach der Apostelgeschichte des Lukas', *NTS* 31, 1985, 437–51.

of belief in the resurrection (23:6; 24:21; 26:6f.; 28:20). When Luke expressly depicts belief in the resurrection as the concern and hope of the people, he can say that, by accusing Paul, his judges have placed themselves outside the people and Judaism. Paul is not an apostate; the leaders of the Jews are: Paul, not his accusers, has the right to speak on behalf of the people and to represent Israel. With his knowledge of the law and his belief in the Messiah, Paul is the real Pharisee and the true Jew who has the right to serve as the teacher of Israel, as he is described in the synagogue scenes in chapters 13–19 and finally in the scene at Rome (28:17ff.). It is commonly held that Luke's real concern in his description of the trial is the conflict between Judaism and Christianity based on the Gentile mission. In chapters 22–6 Paul is really only a cipher for the Gentile mission. If this is correct, we have in Acts 22 and 26 a renewed justification of the Gentile mission based on Jesus' direct command to Paul. Thus chapters 22–6 are in part theologically a repetition of chapters 10, 11 and 15.

This is hardly correct. None of the formulated charges allude to the Gentile mission, but only to what Paul had taught Jews. Luke does not trace the origin of the Gentile mission back to visionary experiences, but to Scripture as the Lord opened it to the disciples, and to the command of the Lord (Luke 24:46f.; Acts 1:8; 13:47). A special revelation is required only to institute the circumcision-free form of the Gentile mission (Acts 10–11). Paul in Acts is first of all a missionary to the Jews and the founder of churches with Gentile-Christian God-fearers (9:15,20; further the synagogue scenes in Acts 13–14; 16:16ff.; 28:17ff.).

It is not necessary for Luke to furnish justification for the Gentile mission once again in chapters 22ff. Luke's theology and composition offer the solution. He has worked out the emergence of a restored Israel, consisting of repentant Jews who are faithful adherents to the law. They possess the distinguishing mark of the people of God, circumcision, and they live according to the law of Israel. Herein lies the significance of the Jewish character of the Jerusalem congregation as it is described in the first part of Acts. The prophecies of

salvation are fulfilled to this restored Israel and, through the
restored people, Gentiles receive a share in God's salvation.
This is how Luke conceives the identity of the church and the
place of Jewish Christians. Luke faces, however, a great
problem in connection with this idea about the identity of the
church, that is what is reported about Paul's teaching concerning the law, Moses and the people.

Paul assumes a dominant position in Acts and most of the
churches stem from his work. Luke reckons on the whole with a
Pauline church. Paul is accused of being a leader of the 'sect of
the Nazarenes' (Acts 24:5). The charges directed against Paul
thus apply to the whole church; the church is involved in the
charge of apostasy, desertion from the chosen people. Paul's
special status in the church beside the Twelve rests on a special
commission from the God of Israel (Acts 22:14), something
attested by a man in the synagogue who is recognized to be
devout according to the law (22:12). The status of Paul has to be
defended, for if the greatest part of the church stems from a
Jewish apostate, the church is not the restored Israel. The
Twelve and Paul represent Israel, while the unrepentant Jews
no longer have claim to the designation 'Israel'. Luke's concern
is the struggle for the right of citizenship in the people of God.

In Luke's presentation of Paul importance is attached to the
guarantees for the truth and legitimacy of his proclamation and
teaching, and here Scripture plays the main role: everything
Paul preaches is found in the Scriptures.[174] This has to do with
the main theme in Luke's picture of Paul, namely Paul as a Jew.
The second theme is Paul as a visionary, charismatic preacher,
healer and miracle-worker (13:8ff.; 14:2ff.; 16:16ff.; 19:11ff.;
20:7ff.; 28:1ff.). Paul's life and work are encompassed with
exorcisms, healings, raisings of the dead and other miracles of
various kinds. Paul's work is determined by the Spirit (9:17;
13:2,4,9; 16:6,7,10ff.,18; 19:1,21; 20:22,23; 21:11), and Paul is, as
are the Twelve, capable of giving the Spirit to other Christians
(19:6). Paul's activity is guided directly from heaven, by God, by
Jesus, or by the Spirit, with the help of visions, auditions,

---

[174] See above, the section 'The Scriptures', particularly pp. 67–8.

different ecstatic experiences, heavenly inspiration etc. We have seven miracles of Paul in Acts (13:4–12; 14:8–10; 16:16–18; 19:13–20; 20:7–12; 28:1–6,7–8). The cumulative reports give the impression that Paul's previous and his future activity is marked by miracles (14:3; 15:12; 19:11–20; 21:19).

That miracles occur everywhere is not to accent Paul's miraculous activity as such, but to say something about his preaching. The miracle is not calculated to rescue Paul in sufferings and persecution, but to exhibit the proclamation as an irresistible force. The retributive miracle against Elymas at Cyprus is calculated to remove a hindrance to the proclamation, and is a part of the teaching of the Lord (13:7f.,12). Against the resistance of the unbelieving Jews in Iconium God himself confirms his word, 'granting signs and wonders to be done by their hands' (14:3). In Acts 4:25–31, boldness for preaching God's word comes through God's permitting healings, miracles and signs to occur through Jesus (4:29–30). In Acts 14:11–18 the primacy of the word is evident, since the miracle can lead to misunderstandings when isolated from the proclamation. The connection between miracle and word is clear (see also Acts 16:16–18 and 19:13–20). When Acts 15:12 sums up the entire missionary activity of Barnabas and Paul in miraculous deeds, the missionary proclamation in Acts 13–14 is presupposed. Luke's composition as a whole allows no separation of miracle and word. Paul's miracles comprise a secondary part of his preaching and teaching, and so the proclamation is legitimized as the word of God.

The miracles are worked and determined by the Spirit of God, and so the Spirit confirms Paul's proclamation. The synagogue did not possess the Spirit. The Spirit is given to the people of God (Acts 2:17ff.), and because the unbelieving Israel does not have the Spirit it does not belong to the people of God: therefore the Jews are not capable of performing miracles. This feature is given special emphasis by the inverted miracle stories: the alleged miracle-worker fails completely. In 19:13–20, the miracle-working of the four sons of the high priest Sceva totally miscarries, as the demon shows itself superior. The Jews are incapable of performing miracles, that is they no longer

have divine authority. We encounter a similar story in the
report in 13:6–12. Elymas, the Jew, is regarded as a miracle-
worker and prophet (13:6), and attempts to frustrate faith in
Jesus (13:8); but his alleged miraculous power is completely
unmasked. He fails with Paul, and is himself struck blind by
Paul's miraculous power (13:11–12).[175] Luke sets forth the frailty
of the synagogue by making clear that it cannot perform any
miracles, but also that the Jews fail totally in their attempt to
perform them. The church, on the other hand, is legitimized, as
its proclamation is legitimized by the miracles.

The guarantees for the Pauline proclamation are given
through the Scriptures and the miracles performed by the
Spirit. And it is the Spirit of the Scriptures that is working
through the miracles and confirms the kerygma.

SALVATION

The significance of the Jesus-event is, first and foremost,
salvation. The saviour is God himself and salvation is God's
own gift (Acts 28:28; Luke 1:47; 2:30; 3:6). Salvation is a part of
the history of the people of God, who has repeatedly acted as
saviour throughout the history of Israel. This history is
therefore the history of salvation, as in Acts 7:2–53 and 13:16–26
(cf. Luke 1:46–55,68–79), whereas in the history of the nations,
that is the Gentiles, God has not acted as saviour (Acts 14:16;
17:25f.). Salvation is a divine prerogative. Israel had saviours
sent to them, like Abraham, Moses and David (Acts 7:7ff.,25,35;
13:17ff.): the last link in that chain is Jesus, to whom God in the
end of times has transferred the divine prerogative of salvation.

The words used for salvation and saviour in Luke–Acts,
sōzein, sōtēria, sōtēr, may derive from two backgrounds, the
Greek world and the Old Testament. In the first, salvation
means the bestowal of various blessings and gifts,[176] while in

---

[175] Luke is aware that miracles can take place outside the church, but, if they do, Luke
      regards them as magic and witchcraft, as is the case with Simon Magus, Acts 8:9ff.

[176] W. Foerster, 'sōzō and sōtēria in the Greek World', *TDNT* VII, 966–80; F.W.
      Danker, *Luke*, Proclamation Commentaries, Philadelphia ² 1987, 28–45, 82–99,
      finds the Greek sense primary for Luke: salvation is the bestowal of any divine gift
      from 'benefactors', saviours.

the Old Testament it means primarily deliverance from
enemies.[177] The reason for not being able to give a precise
definition is that Luke mostly speaks of salvation in general
terms, that is without describing the exact content (cf. Acts
2:21,40,47; 4:12; 5:31; 11:14; 13:23,26,47; 15:1,11; 16:17,30f.). Luke
presupposes that his readers know what salvation means and
that it contains various elements hard to put into one simple
formula.[178] For Luke it is more important to establish that
salvation occurs now, who the saviour is and where salvation is
to be found.

God has transferred the divine prerogatives in salvation to
Jesus (Acts 4:12; 5:31; 13:23; Luke 1:47,69,77; 2:11). The programmatic saying in Acts 4:12 has a polemical tone: 'There is no
salvation in anyone else at all, for there is no other name under
heaven granted to men, by which we may receive salvation.'
Here salvation is the healing of a crippled man (Acts 3:1–10):
the name plays a decisive role in the healing (3:6; 4:7,12,17,18).
The situation of the intended listeners is that they have rejected
and killed God's Messiah (3:13f.). Luke therefore has to show
Jesus' authority to heal, that is to save. This authority is
bestowed upon Jesus by the God of Israel, the only one who has
the right to give salvation: 'The God of Abraham, Isaac, and
Jacob, the God of our fathers, has given the highest honour to
his servant Jesus ...' (3:13). The polemic is addressed not to
Gentiles and their gods and saviours, but to Jews, who denied
that Jesus had any right whatsoever to offer salvation (cf. Luke
5:21ff.), and who had other institutions, other persons and other
names for the saviour. So Luke, being aware that some Jewish
Christians applied salvation even to the name of Moses (Acts

---

[177] For the Old Testament background plead G. Voss, *Die Christologie der lukanischen
Schriften in Grundzügen*, SN 2, Paris/Bruges 1965, 45–60, and P. Minear, *To Heal and
to Reveal. The Prophetic Vocation According to Luke*, New York 1975, 102–11. The primary
benefit is in any case the forgiveness of sins, and here the Old Testament
background is clear: J.A. Fitzmyer, *The Gospel According to Luke*, I, 223f.

[178] J.A. Fitzmyer, ibid., 222: ' "Salvation" denotes the deliverance of human beings
from evil, physical, moral, political, or cataclysmic ... As applied to the Christ
event, the wholeness to which human beings are restored is a sound relation to
God himself. That would imply a rescue from sin, the state of alienation from God
and, in terms of a post-NT theology, a deliverance from eternal damnation'. This
definition could apply to any New Testament writer and therefore even to Luke.

15:1ff.), obviously in addition to Jesus' name (cf. 13:39), removes, for his Jewish-Christian readers, any doubt that Jesus actually was the saviour. This explains the Lucan theologoumenon that Jesus was a suffering Messiah: 'The Messiah must suffer and rise from the dead' (Luke 24:45, further Acts 3:18; 17:3; 26:23; Luke 24:26[179]). Jesus prays: 'Yet not my will, but thine be done' (Luke 22:42). Jesus is aware that he has to perish in Jerusalem (Luke 13:33). The problem is that the doubt has arisen whether Jesus was 'the one to liberate Israel', whether he was the Messiah (Luke 24:21), and this has to do with the suffering of Messiah, his crucifixion and death (24:20). The problem is not the soteriological significance of Jesus' death, with which Luke is familiar, but the identity of the Messiah. It is therefore not sufficient to speak of the death of Jesus as a misunderstanding on the part of the Jews, or because of their ignorance of the Scriptures. This would have meant a blow to Luke's notion of Jesus as the Messiah and Saviour of Israel, even if Luke repeatedly urges that the responsibility for Jesus' death falls on the Jews (Acts 2:23; 3:15; 4:10; 5:30; 7:52; 10:39; 13:27f.). It is therefore necessary to demonstrate that Jesus' suffering and death were in accordance with God's will and his predetermination, and prophesied in the Scriptures (Acts 2:24; 3:18; 13:28–30; 17:3; Luke 9:22,44; 17:25; 18:31–4; 22:22; 24:7,26, 46).[180] The suffering was a 'necessity' (Acts 9:22; 17:25; 22:37; 24:7,26,44; Luke 17:3).[181]

In accordance with the idea that the history of Israel is the history of God's saving acts, salvation through Messiah-Jesus at the end of times can be found only in Israel, that is in the church. The message of this salvation has been sent to the 'stock of Abraham' (13:26, cf. Luke 19:9); the man from David's

---

[179] *Pathein* signifies to Luke the sufferings, crucifixion and death of Jesus (Luke 9:22; 17:25; 22:15; 24:26,46; Acts 1:3; 3:18; 9:16; 17:3).

[180] It is important for Luke to find evidence for the suffering of the Messiah in 'Moses', 'all the prophets' and all the Scriptures (Luke 24:27,46; Acts 13:27,29; 17:3; 26:23; see above, the section 'The Scriptures'). But we have nowhere in the Old Testament or in Jewish literature prior to the New Testament any suffering Messiah. The idea of a suffering Servant of Yahweh in Isa. 52:13 – 53:12 was interpreted in a messianic sense much later than the NT itself.

[181] This is expressed by the impersonal verb *dei*, 'it is necessary that ...', which is frequently used in Luke–Acts.

posterity is brought to Israel as a saviour (13:23, cf. Luke 1:69,77). All Israel has to accept as certain that God has made Jesus both Lord and Messiah (Acts 2:36–41, cf. Luke 2:11). Israel is granted repentance and forgiveness of sins (Acts 5:31). Incorporation and participation in the people of God is necessary for salvation, therefore God added to the church day by day those whom he was saving (2:47, cf. 2:41). The salvation offered to Israel is opened even for Gentiles, peoples who are strangers to the community of Israel and outside God's covenant. Even for Gentiles salvation is to be found in Israel. In the first sermon to Gentiles (Acts 10:34–43), Peter tells his audience that Jesus commanded the apostles to proclaim him to Israel, and that the Gentiles are being involved in the salvation given to the people of God: the salvation is open to all people, but only via Israel. In James' speech at the Apostolic Council (Acts 15:13–23), he makes clear the situation of Jews and Gentiles with regard to salvation by means of a quotation, in vv. 16–18, of Amos 9:11: God will first rebuild and restore Israel, and then, as a result of this event, the Gentiles will seek the Lord. The Cornelius story is cited as proof that the restoration of the fallen house of David has already occurred as well as the Gentiles' seeking the Lord. The 'restoration of the fallen house of David' has taken place in the church, the Jewish-Christian community which is Israel at the end of times, and the Gentiles have gained a share in the salvation that has been given to Israel.

Salvation is linked exclusively with Jesus (Acts 2:21; 4:12; 13:23; 16:31; Luke 1:69; 2:11; 19:9). However, the details are not absolutely clear in this connection. This is why Luke can connect the same effects of salvation with different parts of Jesus' life and work, his death, and his resurrection and ascension. So, for example, the forgiveness of sins is connected with the life of Jesus (Luke 5:21; 7:47), with his death (Luke 24:46–7) and with his resurrection (Acts 2:38; 5:31). That means that you cannot isolate any single phase; rather the whole sweep is redemptive.[182] Above all, salvation is connected with the resurrection as God's saving act for his Messiah (Acts

---

[182] R. Glöckner, *Die Verkündigung des Heils beim Evangelisten Lukas*, Mainz 1976.

2:25–8; 13:37). The forgiveness of sins is given through the
resurrection (Acts 2:38; 3:19; 5:30f.; 10:43; 13:38; 22:16; 26:18;
Luke 24:47), and so is the Holy Spirit (Acts 2:38). Through the
resurrected one, the sick are saved, cured (Acts 3:15ff.; 4:10ff.).
Salvation means even to be rescued from the evil of the people,
Israel, as well as from the evil of the Gentiles (Acts 2:40; 26:17).
The life and work of Jesus also have saving effects. His life
means healing and deliverance from the devil (Acts 10:38; Luke
4:18; 7:20ff.; 17:15f.). Further, it means the forgiveness of sins
(Luke 5:21ff.; 7:47). Salvation is also spoken of in a more general
way, that is without giving any significant idea of its content
(Luke 2:11; 19:9).

The most discussed problem is whether the death of Jesus has
saving significance in Acts. It is clear that Luke does not regard
Jesus' death as a sacrifice or as an expiation for sin. But Luke
knows about the sacrificial death of Jesus; so Acts 20:28: '... the
church of God, which he acquired through the blood of his
Own'.[183] This alludes to the death of Jesus as an atonement,
but, apart from the mere mention, this has no further significance for Luke. In addition we have sacrificial nuances in the
words pronounced at the Last Supper: 'This is my body, which
is given for you' (Luke 22:19);[184] 'this cup, poured out for you, is
the new covenant in my blood' (Luke 22:20). Luke is aware of
the sacrificial death of Jesus and does not deny it, but thrusts it
into the background for some inscrutable reason. But even if
Jesus' death as expiation for sin is of no significance for him, the
death of Jesus nevertheless has saving significance: Acts 13:28–
30 states that the death of Christ was related to God's salvific
plan; Jesus' death is implied as being God's will (Luke 13:33;
17:25; Acts 3:18); we have a series of sayings on the sufferings of
Jesus as a divine 'necessity' (Acts 3:18; 13:28–30; 17:3; Luke
17:25; 24:26,44); the preaching of the forgiveness of sins is the
outcome of the resurrection *and* the death of Christ (Luke
24:46–47). The situation is that Luke clearly connects salvation
with the death of Christ, but he does not say what the death is

---

[183] That no direct soteriological significance is drawn from Jesus' death is a widespread
opinion.

[184] Luke is the only Synoptist who has preserved those sacrificial words.

intended to accomplish.[185] It suffices for him to say that the death of Christ is part of the redemption.

When Luke sums up what salvation is all about, the most important element is 'the forgiveness of sins', *aphesis hamartiōn*.[186] The verbal form, 'to forgive sins', is found repeatedly in Luke's Gospel,[187] but throughout Acts, and three times in the Gospel, we have the abstract form, *aphesis hamartiōn*,[188] which means that God has cancelled the 'debt of guilt incurred by their evil conduct'.[189]

In the great commission to the eleven the forgiveness of sins is used as the heading to the whole of Christ's work and to the proclamation: 'This, he said, is what is written: that the Messiah is to suffer death and to rise from the dead on the third day, and that in his name repentance bringing the forgiveness of sins is to be proclaimed to all nations, beginning from Jerusalem' (Luke 24:46–7). All the occurrences of *aphesis* in Acts we find in the same type of context, namely in speeches to Jews and about Jews. The forgiveness is the last chance for the people and likely to happen only once, which means that when the mission has come to the end of the earth, that is the Dispersion, there will be no more salvation for Israel. In the speech on the day of Pentecost, Peter tells the Jews who crucified Christ (Acts 2:36) to repent and so obtain forgiveness of sins (2:38). Because the Jews had repudiated the Messiah, Peter tells them to repent and return to God to have their sins wiped out (Acts 3:13f.,19). God has granted Israel repentance and forgiveness of sins after they had done Jesus to death (Acts 5:30f.; 13:28,38). The people and their evil deeds against Jesus

---

185 Different models have been suggested: martyrdom in itself as redemptive; cf. W.E. Pilgrim, 'The Death of Jesus in Lucan Soteriology', dissertation, Princeton 1971; G. Schneider, *Verleugnung, Verspottung und Verhör Jesu nach Lukas 22:54–71*, StANT 22, 1969; G. Voss, *Die Christologie der lukanischen Schriften in Grundzügen*; Jesus' death as the foiled temptation of the 'new Adam', R. Karris, *Luke: Artist and Theologian. Luke's Passion Account as Literature*, New York 1985; J. Neyrey, *The Passion according to Luke: A Redaction Study of Luke's Soteriology*, New York 1985.

186 *Aphesis* is used in the Septuagint and in Greek for release from debt and release from captivity; the association of the word with 'sin' is from Jewish religion, where 'debt' is used in the sense of sin.

187 5:11,20,21,23,24; 7:47,48,49; 11:4, cf. 12:10; 17:3f.

188 We have eleven occurrences in the New Testament; Luke alone has eight.

189 J.A. Fitzmyer, *The Gospel According to Luke* I, 224.

are addressed in Acts 10:39,43 and 26:18,[190] but here Gentiles too are included in the proclamation to Israel. Luke uses *hamartia* in Acts only in the cases mentioned.[191] And so, when Luke talks about the forgiveness of sins, he is dealing with the Jewish guilt in the death of Jesus, that is their sin – he is talking about this great sin and the one great repentance in the history of the people; there seems to be only one. Thus, salvation can mean to be rescued from the sinful people and from evil Gentiles (2:40; 26:17), or even to be a member of the repentant Israel (2:41; 26:18). Sin is not, as it is for Paul, sinful existence and sin understood as power, but the evil deeds against God's Messiah. The sins are not seen from a moralistic point of view, but have to do with the relation to God. The sins have been there throughout the history of the people (Acts 7:2–53; Luke 1:77; 3:3), but the climax and the last sin of the people is seen in the reaction to the Jesus-event, and even here we have the last saving act of God. The forgiveness of sins is the prerogative of God,[192] who in this way restores the relationship with his people. With the forgiveness of sins and repentance and faith[193] as the essential conditions, salvation also has other connotations, denoting deliverance from various evils: so salvation means healing (Acts 4:9f.; 14:9; Luke 6:7; 7:50; 8:48,50 etc.), peace as the mark of the messianic kingdom (Acts 10:36; Luke 2:14; 19:38,42; 24:36 etc.), and life (Acts 5:20; Luke 10:25ff.). [194]

THE PEOPLE OF GOD IN THE EMPIRE

The church lives in the Roman Empire and Luke is fully aware of the problems involved in this situation. The part played by the Empire in the death of Jesus is described in the prayer in Acts 4:27–30:

[190] In this case the sinner is Paul, 26:15; v. 18 applies to Jews *and* Gentiles, but Paul is above all sent to the Jews, cf. Acts 22:16.

[191] The exception is Stephen (Acts 7:60), but even here it has to do with the sins of the Jews.

[192] This is clear even in 5:20ff., where the verb is passive.

[193] Acts 13:39; 14:9; 16:31; Luke 7:50; 8:12,48,50; 17:19; 18:42 etc.

[194] For other modes of expressing the effects of the Christ-event: J.A. Fitzmyer, *The Gospel According to Luke* I, 226f.

For of a truth against thy holy child Jesus, whom thou hast anointed, both Herod, and Pontius Pilate, with the Gentiles, and the people of Israel, were gathered together, for to do whatsoever thy hand and thy counsel determined before to be done. And now, Lord, behold their threatenings: and grant unto thy servants, that with all boldness they may speak thy word, by stretching forth thine hand to heal; and that signs and wonders may be done by the name of thy holy child Jesus.

Herod and Pilate are both responsible for the death of Jesus, and they have acted together with the Gentiles, the Roman soldiers and the people[195] of Israel. Enmity with Jesus unites Gentiles and Jews: the Jews co-operate with the enemies of Israel and God against the God of Israel and his Messiah; the Roman Empire represents the Gentiles in hostility against the Messiah of God.[196] The undertaking of the Jews and the Empire is futile as they only achieve what God has foreordained. In the passion of Jesus, God's will and power were revealed. The political authorities of Jews and Gentiles are a threat to the church (4:29), but the answer to the threat is the God-given ability to preach the gospel with all boldness, and the healings, signs and wonders by the hand of God. The situation for the church in the Roman Empire is thus clear.

In the light of the clear and programmatic text of Acts 4:25ff., it is surprising to find that most exegetes understand Luke's purpose in Acts as political apology for Christianity, directed against the Roman Empire; the evidence is found above all in the lawsuit against Paul (Acts 22–8). The speeches of Paul in this part of Acts are of an apologetic nature, but what kind of apologetic? Surely not a political one. There are various forms

---

[195] The plural is conspicuous, but has to do with the plural 'peoples' in the quotation from Ps. 2 in v. 25.

[196] Luke repeatedly points to the Jews as responsible for the death of Jesus (Acts 2:23; 3:14f.; 4:10; 7:52; 10:39; 13:27f.). Apart from 4:27, the Romans and Pilate are mentioned in connection with the death of Jesus at 2:23: the Jews murdered Jesus 'through the hand of the lawless', that is Gentiles; see further Acts 13:28: the Jews asked Pilate to have Jesus executed. E. Haenchen, *Acts*, 228, finds the verdict passed on Pilate at odds with Luke's theology; so even D. Bock, *Proclamation from Prophecy*, 205: the text is traditional, cf. further H. Conzelmann, *Acts*, 35. It is clear that we have tensions between 4:27f. and Luke 23:1,5, where Pilate is apologetically exonerated. Why did Luke employ such a tradition? There is a different view of the Romans in Acts from that in Luke's passion story, and the view in 4:27ff. coincides with the picture of the Romans later in Acts.

of the idea of a political apology, mostly understood as an appeal to the Romans for toleration. Luke seeks to show that Christianity must have the same privileges as the Jewish religion had in the Empire as 'permitted religion', *religio licita*, and the church, then, is seen as a part of Judaism and the true successor to Israel.[197] Luke tries to persuade Roman outsiders that Christianity is politically harmless;[198] Luke wants to subdue the apprehension of the Romans concerning the Christian mission;[199] Luke offers an *apologia pro imperio* to the church;[200] the Christians shall live at peace with the sovereign power;[201] the purpose is to demonstrate to Roman Christians that faith in Jesus and allegiance to Rome are not mutually incompatible.[202]

It is an issue in itself that the state and the Roman Empire are never dealt with in principle. Nothing like a *religio licita* has ever existed.[203] The Romans treated foreign religions not in a framework of a doctrine of 'permitted religion', but on an *ad hoc* basis. The Jews actually had some privileges,[204] but this was necessitated 'in the main by the anti-Semitism of Alexandria and of other Greek cities and by the desirability of avoiding disorders which might arise if it was not officially restrained ...'[205]

It is hard to find any connection between the presumed political apology in Acts 22–6 and the preceding portions of Acts, above all with Acts 4:25ff. If the speeches in Acts 22–6 are to be understood as political apologetic, this portion of Acts is left hanging in the air and appears to be an appendage. Politics are not thereby excluded, but other factors demonstrate the

---

[197] Above all, B.S. Easton, *Early Christianity*, Greenwich, CT, 1955 (= *The Purpose of Acts*, London 1936) 41ff.; further: *Beg.* II, 177–87.

[198] H. Conzelmann, *Theology of St Luke*, 144.

[199] F. Bovon, *Lukas* I, EKK III/1, 23.

[200] P.W. Walaskay, *'And so we came to Rome': The Political Perspective of St Luke*, SNTSMS 49, Cambridge 1983.

[201] R. Maddox, *The Purpose of Luke–Acts*, FRLANT 126, Göttingen 1982, 97.

[202] P. Esler, *Community and Gospel*, 210.

[203] H. Conzelmann, *Theology of St Luke*, 144–8; *Acts*, xlvii; P. Esler, *Community and Gospel*, 211ff.; R. Maddox, *Purpose*, 91–3.

[204] P. Esler, *Community and Gospel*, 211ff.; H.W. Tajra, *The Trial of St Paul*, WUNT 35, Tübingen 1989, 15–21.

[205] A.D. Nock, 'Religious Developments from the Close of the Republic to the Death of Nero', in *The Cambridge Ancient History* X, 1934, 490–2.

improbability of this idea. First of all, Acts 4:27f. is a rather strange, provocative and most unlikely introduction to an appeal to Roman authorities for a friendly attitude towards Christians. The theological argumentation in the presumably political-apologetic speeches is unintelligible to Roman authorities,[206] but not to Christians, and the addressees of Acts are obviously Christians, not Roman officials. The way Luke in fact portrays the Romans is decisive evidence against the thesis of assumed attempts by him to describe the Romans as positively as possible and as very tolerant of the church; they frequently appear in an unflattering light. This is so even before the description of the lawsuit: Paul was beaten and imprisoned illegally (Acts 16:22f.,35–37); Gallio refuses to countenance a charge against Paul, but tolerates a disgraceful treatment of Sosthenes in front of the tribunal (18:12–17). The two main Roman characters, the governors Felix and Festus, are partial and led by Jewish interests (Acts 25:9–11). Felix, who was well informed about Christianity and married to a Jew, is downright corrupt (24:22,26); he solicits bribes from Paul and, in order to obtain personal gain from the Jews, he leaves Paul in prison against his better judgement and contrary to Roman law (Acts 24:27). In spite of Paul being proven innocent the Romans do not release him, but keep him illegitimately in prison (24:22,27; 25:4,7,9,18,25; 26:32). The prisoner Paul gives the governor Festus a summing up and exposes him as a liar (25:10–11). The governor is lying when he refers to his own role in the trial (Acts 25:16–17,25 and 25:1–12). Paul's Roman citizenship and his appeal to Caesar save him from the Jewish plot against his life as well as from the greed and corrupt political man-oeuvring of the Roman officials, since with the appeal the affair is taken out of the hands of the provincial officials (22:25ff.; 23:27; 25:9ff.). The reason for his appeal is not that he trusted the imperial court rather than the Sanhedrin in Jerusalem – Jews and Gentile Romans make common cause.

---

[206] C.K. Barrett, *Luke the Historian in Recent Study*, London 1961, 63: 'theological and ecclesiastical rubble ...' Luke expresses this clearly by having the governor Festus request the Jewish king Agrippa for help in order to gain even the slightest notion about what is going on, Acts 25:24 – 26:3.

Paul never indicates that he expects justice from the emperor; he does not count on a favourable outcome of the trial and the trial never comes to an end. Not even here are the Romans put in a favourable light. When sending Paul to Rome, the governor is not able to indicate the charges against him (25:26f.). This shows that Luke's apologetic speeches are part of an intra-Jewish debate; Luke defends Paul against Jewish and Jewish-Christian accusations.

In the lawsuit against Paul the charges against him have to do with his alleged teaching against Israel, the law and the temple (Acts 21:21,28; 24:5; 25:8; 28:17). On some occasions charges of sedition have been raised, which come mostly from Jews (Acts 17:6f.; 24:5). The Romans have accused him of civil disturbances (Acts 16:20; 21:38; 25:8). There are obviously political concerns involved: this is clear from Luke's idea of the church as the restored Israel, from his christology with Jesus as the Messiah-king and from his eschatology about the kingdom of God. In Luke's description of the trial and execution of Jesus there is a political concern, as indicated by the charge brought against Jesus in Luke 23:2: 'We found this man subverting our nation, opposing the payment of the taxes to Caesar, and claiming to be Messiah, a King'.[207] Jesus was crucified as the king of the Jews (Luke 23:38). The political concern is clear in the charge brought forward in Thessalonica, in Acts 17:7: 'They all flout the emperor's laws, saying that there is another king, Jesus'. Luke denies the charges and emphasizes that the Christian leaders were not guilty of subversion (Acts 16:37; 18:14f.; 24:12; 25:18; 26:32), but rather that they have been the victims of conspiracy. The reason for this emphasis is not meant as a 'demonstration that Christian preaching does not impinge upon the power of the Empire'.[208] Luke is not asking for the favour of the Romans on behalf of the church. Acts is not addressed to the Jews or Roman officials, but Christians. Luke is far from any idea of endorsing the authority of the

[207] Luke phrases the charge to emphasize its political nature and at the same time underlines its falsity. Cf. John 19:12–15.

[208] H. Conzelmann, *Acts*, xlvii. The idea that Luke's attitude to the state has to do with the delay of the parousia, so H. Conzelmann, *Theology of St Luke*, 149, is false.

Empire.[209] Luke's intention is to show Christians that the Empire cannot mean any serious threat to the church, cannot obstruct the proclamation of the gospel and is forced to serve the will of God, even if it joins with the Jews in persecuting the church. At the crucifixion of Jesus the Romans joined with the Jews against God, but only 'to do whatever thy hand and thy plan had predestined to take place' (Acts 4:27f.). It was the deliberate will and plan of God that the Jews should use the Romans to kill Jesus (Acts 2:23, cf. 13:28). The same idea is to be found in the description of the lawsuit against Paul and his appeal to the emperor.

From the very beginning, God's will is that the witness of the church shall reach to 'the ends of the earth', namely Rome (Acts 1:8).[210] Paul is the one chosen by God for this. Paul is going to Rome not on his own initiative, but according to God's will and plan, *dei* (Acts 19:21). The Lord appeared to Paul in jail, encouraging him and declaring his will: 'You have testified of me in Jerusalem, and you must (*dei*) bear witness also in Rome' (Acts 23:11). The Holy Spirit testified that Paul should be handed over to the Romans (21:11). An angel declared to Paul that it was ordained by God (*dei*) that Paul should appear in Rome (Acts 27:24). And so the meaning of the behaviour of the Romans in the lawsuit is clear: whatever their intentions, they are forced by God to bring Paul and the gospel to Rome. Paul's appeal to the emperor is not in order to get a fair trial. He never appears in court, and it is not necessary for Luke to say anything further about the trial. Paul witnesses in Rome (Acts 28:17ff.), so that God's will from the beginning is carried through, even by the Empire.

The answer from the church to the authorities is not any kind of political action. The emphasis on the innocence of the Christian leaders is seriously meant. Acts 4:28–9 makes it clear

---

[209] And he is very far from the ideas of Paul in Rom. 13:1ff.

[210] Otherwise: E. Ellis, '"Das Ende der Erde" (Apg 1,8)', in C. Bussmann and W. Radl (eds.), *Der Treue Gottes trauen: Beiträge zum Werk des Lukas für Gerhard Schneider*, Freiburg/Basle/Vienna 1991, 277–88; M. Hengel, 'Der Historiker Lukas und die Geographie Palästinas in der Apostelgeschichte', *ZDPV* 99, 1983, 153f.; C.W. van Unnik, 'Der Ausdruck 'ΕΩΣ 'ΕΣΧΑΤΟΥ ΤΗΣ ΓΗΣ (Apg 1:8) und sein alttestamentlicher Hintergrund', in *Sparsa Collecta* I, Leiden 1973, 386–401.

that the only response the church is to give is the proclamation
of the word of God accompanied by healings and miracles. The
Christians have to put up with false accusations and persecutions (Acts 14:22) for the sake of the gospel. Luke knows very
well that all the kingdoms of the world are of the devil (Luke
4:5f.).[211] He has a contemptuous disregard of rulers (Luke
13:1–3,32), and an ironic saying about the title 'Benefactor' used
by Hellenistic kings (Luke 22:24ff.). He does not have an
optimistic view of the Empire, but knows that the church
occasionally has to defy the political authority; hence Acts 4:19
and 5:29, 'We must obey God rather than men'. The authority
in question is not that of the Romans, but formulated as a
principle indicating how the church is to regard any political
authority. The problem in Acts 4 and 5 is the attempt of the
authorities to stop the public preaching of the church (4:18;
5:28), and the response from the church is precisely the
preaching and teaching and nothing else (4:20 and 5:29–32). To
bring the name of Jesus before the authorities is decisive for
relations with the Empire (Acts 9:15; 13:7; 24:14ff.; 26:1–32;
Luke 12:11f.; 21:14f.). No subversion shall take place in the
church, no defiance, no self-assertiveness. Christianity is then
politically harmless, but only for the time being. This is why
Luke knows that when the kingdom of God comes, all the
political powers will stand helpless (Luke 21:20–31). The church
is the heir of the kingdom and the future: 'Have no fear, little
flock; for your Father has chosen to give you the kingdom'
(Luke 12:32).

THE LAST DAYS ARE UPON US

With Jesus the last days begin. Luke is aware that Jesus and the
church signify that the last days have arrived; if this is not the
case then Jesus is not the true Messiah and the Christian
message is not the word of God. The fulfilment of the promises
means that the last days are upon the world. It is therefore a
conditio sine qua non to know the character of the time in which

---

[211] Would Luke have retained and intensified the word from Matt. 4:8f. if his idea was
a political apologetic in order to obtain the favour of the Empire?

the church lives.[212] Eschatology is one of the important dimensions of Luke's work: he sets out to solve the problems regarding eschatology in his Gospel; in Acts he can look back on what he maintained in the former work, but in Acts he is more concerned about the question 'to whom is the kingdom given' than 'when will the kingdom appear'. We have in Acts no discourses on eschatology, but only short references within some speeches. Luke reckoned with an endtime. He did not dismiss the parousia, but affirms that Jesus is to return in the same way as he went to heaven (Acts 1:11, cf. Luke 21:27,36). He acknowledged that Jesus had not returned as early as expected,[213] but he has very ancient eschatological traditions from mission-preaching, unique mentions of the 'times of refreshing' and the 'restoration of all things' (Acts 3:19–21). Is the consummation near or distant for him? Has the present, that is the time of the church, eschatological quality?

The coming of the Holy Spirit upon the disciples at Pentecost is seen as an eschatological event: 'God says, this will happen in the last days: I will pour out upon everyone a portion of my Spirit . . .' (Acts 2:17). Luke has a long quotation from Joel 3:1–5 in Acts 2:17–21. Its unusual length shows the importance of the point being made, and the quotation marks a decisive new turn in history, explicitly connecting the Old Testament and Jewish expectation of the renewal of the Spirit in the age to come with the experiences of the disciples. Luke invokes Joel's apocalyptic speech in order to signify the present time as eschatological. The descriptions of the coming of the Spirit, its effect on the apostles and on the people they spoke to (Acts 2:2, 3,6ff.) are from the eschatological description in Isaiah 66:15ff.: storm, fire, nations and languages. The Joel text from the Septuagint

---

[212] Eschatology is a most difficult and controverted aspect of Lucan theology today. This has to do with the proposal, above all, of H. Conzelmann, *Theology of St Luke*, that Luke recasts the prophecy of Jesus about the imminent end, so that the envisaged end to world history is located in the indefinite future: a 'delay' of the parousia. For the discussion of eschatology in Luke–Acts: F. Bovon, *L'oeuvre de Luc. Etudes d'exégèse et de théologie*, Lectio Divina 130, Paris 1987, 21–84; R. Maddox, *Purpose*, 100–57. Among scholars there is a serious division of opinions: the delayed eschatology, individual eschatology, imminent eschatology, future eschatology, present eschatology.

[213] E.g. 1 Thess. 4:15ff.; 1 Cor. 15:51.

has undergone some few modifications, by which Luke emphasizes that the outpouring of the Spirit happens in the last days.
Luke first of all substitutes, in v. 17, 'in the last days'[214] for
Septuagint's 'after these things'.[215] Luke's alteration can only
mean that the turning-point has already taken place, the
expected new age has arrived.[216] Scripture itself proves that the
experiences of the disciples show the dawn of the kingdom of
God; this time and these events are those promised in the
Scriptures. Luke does not intend to say that the end of time
came with the outpouring of the Spirit, but that the whole time
after Jesus' birth is 'the last days'.

The quotation from Joel shows what happens in the last days:
outpouring of the Spirit, prophecy and miracles (vv. 17–19a),
and so the apocalyptic occurrences ending with the day of the
Lord (vv. 19a–20).[217] The last days are a chain of occurrences, a
historical process, ending with the parousia. This corresponds
with the discourse of Jesus in Luke 21:5–28, where Luke
separates, within the eschatological process, intervening historical events (21:5–24)[218] and the apocalyptic occurrences ending
with the day of the Lord (21:25–7). In the speech in Luke 17:20–
37 we find the same separation: the eschatological time, the
kingdom of God, is there with Jesus (17:20–5), but the day of the
Son of Man is the end of the eschatological time (17:26–30).
Nothing is said about how near or distant the day of the Lord
actually is. Nothing points to a long delay of the parousia, so
that the church of Luke's day has to adjust itself to a long
period of persecution. No, the persecutions in themselves are
eschatological signs. Luke 21:31f. points to the near future:
'When you see these things happening, know that the kingdom

214 So ℵ, A, D, E, I, P, S, 462 and others.
215 B, C(al), 076, sa. The reading 'after these things' is today rejected by almost all
interpreters as obviously an assimilation to the Septuagint.
216 The text gives no support for Conzelmann's assertion, *Theology of St Luke*, 87, n.2,
that 'the Spirit Himself is no longer the eschatological gift, but the substitute in the
meantime for the possession of salvation'.
217 This does not mean that Luke in v. 19 has the transition from the non-
eschatological time of the church to the apocalyptic future, so H. Conzelmann,
Acts, 20, but the whole 'time of the church' is eschatological time.
218 Such as the destruction of the temple, wars, earthquakes, famines, persecutions of
the church. The wording anticipates at several points phrases used in Acts.

of God is near. Truly I tell you that this generation will not pass away until all things happen.' This can only mean that the generation of Jesus' contemporaries will not completely die out before 'all these things', that is the eschatological occurrences, including the parousia, have taken place.[219] 'The kingdom of God' is an eschatological term.[220] In the same direction as Luke 21:31f. point the words of Jesus in Luke 9:27: 'There are some standing here who will not taste death until they see the kingdom of God.' This can only mean that the kingdom of God is an event within the lifetime of some of Jesus' hearers.[221] The kingdom of God is here obviously identical with the coming of the Son of Man (9:26). The kingdom of God is always present after Jesus, but the day of his coming lies in the future.

The issue of the kingdom of God in Acts is, for Luke, more 'to whom' than 'when'. This explains why future eschatology in Acts is remarkably reduced in comparison with the Gospel. In the quotation from Joel 3:1–5 in Acts 2:17–21 the outpouring of the Spirit concerns Israel (2:14,17,22,24,29f.,39);[222] in Joel 3–4, in the LXX, the outpouring of the Spirit is connected inseparably with the restoration of Israel,[223] and this is also true in

---

[219] The crucial point is 'this generation'. Many futile attempts have been made to establish another meaning than 'this generation'. See R. Maddox, *Purpose*, 111–15.

[220] 'The kingdom of God' is always employed by Luke as an eschatological term (Luke 9:2; 10:9,11; 11:2; 12:32; 13:29; 14:15; 18:24,25,29; 22:16,18,29f., Acts 1:6; 14:22 etc.). The kingdom is an eschatological entity, in the present (Luke 11:20; 17:20f.), or in its future coming (Luke 9:27; 21:31f.; 22:28–30 etc.). In some of the sayings on the kingdom, the time-reference is not clear, but its eschatological nature is. That Luke uses various expressions in order to replace the proclamation of the nearness of the kingdom with 'timeless expressions of its nature', so H. Conzelmann, *Theology of St Luke*, 114f., is not supported by the texts.

[221] Luke has made two alterations from the wording of his source in Mark 9:1; he has changed the adverb modifying 'standing' from *hode* to *autou* and omitted the phrase 'having come with power'. *Autou* in Acts 18:19 and 21:4 means 'there' rather than 'here'; and so Conzelmann, *Theology of St Luke*, 104f., has suggested that Luke means not those standing where Jesus delivers his teaching, but some standing at another place ('there') at some future time. This is lexicographically unlikely and exegetically impossible. That the omission of 'having come with power' is to avoid Mark's reference to the coming of the kingdom of God as the eschatological climax, 9:1, is unlikely. The time-reference in the text is taken into consideration; it supports the meaning that some will see the kingdom of God because they will still be alive when it comes.

[222] The first time the Spirit is given to a Gentile, that is a God-fearer, is Acts 10:44f.

[223] Joel 3:1–5 and 3:6,26.

Acts. In Jesus' intercourse with the apostles in the forty days
after his resurrection, he spoke to them about the kingdom of
God (Acts 1:3–5). The apostles take it for granted that the
kingdom is something that belongs to Israel: 'Lord, are you at
this time restoring[224] the kingdom to Israel?' (1:6). The apostles
are always connected with the kingdom. In Luke 22:28–30 Jesus
vested in them the kingdom, which the father vested in him,
and the kingdom is the kingdom for Israel (cf. Luke 12:32). This
is clear even in Luke 24:13–27: after the sufferings of Jesus the
disciples had lost their faith in him as the one who should
liberate Israel (24:21), but Jesus overcame their doubts with a
reference to the prophets' witness to the sufferings of the
Messiah before his entering his glory (24:25–7). The resurrected
Jesus is installed on the throne of David, again the kingdom of
Israel (Acts 2:30, cf. Luke 1:32–3,68; 2:38; for the kingdom and
the apostles see further Acts 1:3,5,15–26). The question is no
longer *whether* Jesus will restore the kingdom to Israel, but only
when. We are not dealing with an individual eschatology: that is,
Luke had not reinterpreted eschatology, 'the end', as referring
to what is the fate of the individual's soul at his or her death.[225]
In his answer[226] to the question (1:6), Jesus does not deny that
the kingdom is for Israel,[227] only that it is not for the apostles to
know about dates and times. They will receive the promise

---

[224]   Cf. LXX Isa. 49:6; Dan. 4:36.
[225]   For the view that Luke presented this reinterpretation since the parousia did not
occur within the expected time: J. Dupont, 'Die individuelle Eschatologie im
Lukasevangelium und in der Apostelgeschichte', in *FS J. Schmid*, Freiburg 1973, 37–
47; G. Schneider, *Parusiegleichnisse im Lukasevangelium*, SBS 74, Stuttgart 1975, 78–84,
89f., 94–98.
[226]   The answer is often wrongly seen as evasive, but it is to the point; it is evasive only
if the question concerned whether the kingdom of Israel would be restored, but it
actually concerns the point of time when this was going to happen.
[227]   It is an interpretation tenacious of life that in the question in v. 6 we have to do
with nationalistic and particularistic reminiscences which Jesus indirectly(!) denies.
This is not based on the text, but on the assumption that the Gentile-Christian
Luke writing for Gentile Christians at the end of the century could not possibly
have had such Jewish-Christian ideas. Most of the exegetes find that Luke has Jesus
here denying or correcting the apostles. Otherwise: E. Franklin, *Christ the Lord*,
10,95,102,130; D. Juel, *Luke–Acts. The Promise of History*, Atlanta 1983, 63; A.J. Matill,
Jr, *Luke and the Last Things: A Perspective for the Understanding of Lukan Thought*, Dillsboro,
NC, 1979, 135–45; P. Minear, *To Heal and to Reveal*, 135; D. Tiede, *Prophecy and
History in Luke–Acts*, Philadelphia 1980, 90.

made by the Father (1:5,8), the Holy Spirit, and so they will be witnesses (1:8). This is in itself the eschatological process,[228] leading to the restoration of Israel; the outpouring of the Spirit is no alternative to the kingdom for Israel, but an important part of the restoration process. The restoration is, for Luke, an important part of the promises which now are in the process of being fulfilled. In the birth-narratives the redemption of Israel is presented as prophecy (Luke 1:32ff.,54,68ff.; 2:11,38), in Acts we have the fulfilment; through the resurrection Jesus was raised to sit on David's throne (2:30–6). The subject of the whole work of Luke is 'the things which have been fulfilled among us' (Luke 1:1): Luke's story is the fulfilment of the divine promises to God's people, a fulfilment which, having started in Jesus' lifetime (Luke 4:21), continues to be effective in the proclamation of the church, and this has to do with the restoration of Israel. Paul says in Acts 13:32f.: 'We proclaim to you that the promise God made to the fathers he has fulfilled to us their children.' This has to do with Israel: in Paul's speech in 13:16–41 we have a résumé of the history of Israel, where Jesus is seen as a part of that history and as Israel's saviour (13:17–25); God is 'the God of this people of Israel' (13:17); the 'fathers' are the Israelites (13:17,32,36); the apostles were witnesses before 'our nation' (13:32). Luke talks of fulfilments which have taken place throughout the history of Israel, but the restoration of Israel happens in the last days.

Nothing is said in Acts 1:6ff. about the time for the restoration of the kingdom, but the outpouring of the Spirit takes place after some days, and, as the gift of the Spirit is the presupposition for the proclamation (Acts 1:4,8; Luke 24:48f.), the witnessing of the church is in itself a part of the eschatological process. Then it is possible to say something about the consummation: it will come when the gospel has reached 'to the ends of the earth' (Acts 1:8; Luke 24:47). How near or how

---

[228] The apostles' question had to do with a point of time – *en tō chronō* – but Jesus' answer refers to a period – *chronous e kairous*. In the Gospel Luke uses *kairos* in the singular; the exception is 21:24, 'the times of the Gentiles', that is a period (cf. Acts 3:14,17,19; 17:26). The plural of *chronos* means a period, a lapse of time (Luke 8:29; 20:9; 23:8; Acts 3:21; 17:30); even the singular can mean a lapse of time (Acts 1:21; 8:11; 14:3; 18:20; 20:18).

distant this is to Luke, he does not say, but the fact that he
retains expressions pointing to the parousia as imminently
expected tells us that he does not see it as postponed indefinitely
(Luke 3:7,9; 9:27; 10:9,11; 18:7–8; 21:32f.,36).[229]

As he deals with eschatology, Luke can look back on what is
already fulfilled: the last days are partly history to him, as are
the proclamation of Jesus, his resurrection and ascension, and
the outpouring of the Spirit. Some of the promises are about to
be fulfilled: the work of the Spirit in the church, the proclamation of the fulfilment and the restoration of Israel. And, lastly,
there are some of the promises which will be fulfilled in the
future: that is, the parousia with the consummation.

Luke mentions the parousia only four times, very briefly, in
Acts: 1:11; 3:19–21; 10:42 and 17:31. There is postponement.
Even if Luke here has no particular time-reference, the consummation is obviously not too far away, as it is connected with
and dependent upon the mission to the Jews. When Luke
writes, the gospel has reached most of the Jews even in the
Dispersion, and so the parousia cannot be too far away. More
likely it is imminent. The addressees in the speech in Acts 3:11–
26 are all the people in Jerusalem (3:9,11);[230] they are Israelites
(3:12,13,17,22ff.). The wonder of the healing of the lame man
(3:1–10) is a sign that shows that the time of restoration is near.
As the people of God has killed the Messiah of Israel (3:14f.), it
is necessary for the people to repent and convert. The outcome
will be the blotting out of Israel's sins, and then the 'times of
refreshing' will come from the Lord (3:19). This is the effect of
the coming of the Messiah, Jesus, the one appointed to

---

[229] There is no evidence for the idea that Luke taught not to expect the consummation,
the day of the Lord, in the near future. The texts which have been of special
importance for the question of any delay of the parousia are: Luke 9:27; 13:22–30;
14:15–24; 19:11–27; 21:32; 22:69; Acts 1:6–8. In some of these texts, Luke's concern is
not the point of time for the kingdom of God, but who will be admitted to it (Luke
13:22–30; 14:15–24; 19:11–27). In two texts, Luke 9:27; 21:32, the only possible
meaning is that Jesus, according to Luke, expected the parousia in the future, but
before the death of some of his contemporaries. In the other texts there is no
interest in any teaching of any delay of the kingdom of God.

[230] *Pas ho laos* does not mean the whole population of Jerusalem, but 'the people', that
is Israel as living in Jerusalem, cf. 13:44, *pasa he polis* (in Antioch); 14:3, *hoi te ochloi*;
further 8:6,10.

Israel,[231] sent from God.[232] Jesus has now a time of heavenly session, in itself a sign of his coming to Israel: this is the theological significance of his ascension. The heavenly session lasts until the time of 'the restoration of all things' (3:21). The phrase 'times of refreshing' (3:20), in itself apocalyptic language,[233] means ' the restoration of all things' (3:21). The word *apokatastasis* we find only here in the New Testament, but Luke uses *apokathistēmi*[234] in Acts 1:6 for the restoration of the kingdom to Israel. We have the same meaning here.[235] First, the addressees are the people of Israel gathered in Jerusalem (3:9,11,12,17); they are the sons of the prophets and within the covenant of God with Israel (3:25). Second, the God here acting is the God of Israel (3:13ff.). And third, Moses and all the prophets have predicted these days in the end of time and what is going to happen: the coming of the prophet of Israel, the extirpation of the disobedient from the people and the blessing of all Israel (3:21–6).[236]

Jesus' coming on the cloud is mentioned very briefly (Acts 1:10–11). The verses seem to be an unnecessary insertion, as they represent a break in a very clear coherent text, 1:1–9,12–14. The emphasis in the text is on the teaching of Jesus to his apostles in the forty days between his resurrection and

---

[231] The verb *procheirizomai* appears only in Acts in the New Testament (22:14; 26:6, cf. 10:41; 15:7).

[232] A sending of Jesus at the end of times is not known to the New Testament, but is a very archaic, pre-lucan conception: cf. F. Hahn, *Christologische Hoheitstitel*, FRLANT 83, Göttingen ³ 1966, 180ff.; 'Das Problem alter christologischer Überlieferungen in der Apostelgeschichte unter besonderer Berücksichtigung von Act 3,19–21', in J. Kremer (ed.), *Les Actes des Apôtres. Traditions, rédaction, théologie*, BETL 48, Leuven 1979, 131ff.

[233] 4 Ezra 11:46; 2 Bar. 73:1–74:1; Heb. 3:11; 4:9,11.

[234] As an eschatological term Matt. 17:11, the restoration of all through Elijah.

[235] So E. Franklin, *Christ the Lord*, 102; A.J. Matill, Jr., *Luke and the Last Things* 143; D.M. Hamm, 'The Sign of Healing', dissertation, St Louis Univ., Missouri 1975, 220–2, sees the healing in Acts 3:1–10 as an image of the restoration of Israel; see also A.W. Wainwright, 'Luke and the Restoration of the Kingdom to Israel', *ET* 89, 1977, 76–9.

[236] *Hai patriai tēs gēs* can only mean 'all the families on earth', that is Israel. Luke has here altered the phrase *panta ta ethnē* from Septuagint Gen. 22:18. *Patriai* in the Septuagint means 'family, tribe', and it stands always for Israel. Of the three occurrences in the New Testament Luke has two; in Luke 2:4 it means the family of David. The adjective *patrōos*, which only Luke has in the New Testament, and his mentioning 'the fathers' always applies to Israel.

ascension, pointing to what is going to happen imminently, the
outpouring of the Spirit. In this context vv. 10–11, with the
future parousia, seem unimportant and subordinate. Do the
words of the angel, 'Why stand gazing up to heaven?', suggest a
delay of the parousia?[237] If this is so, why is Acts 1:11 not
formulated to point forward to the continuing relationship
between Jesus in heaven and the disciples through the Spirit?
Instead the parousia is mentioned, which gives the context a
clear eschatological tone: the end of times is upon us. Then the
proclamation of the gospel from Jerusalem to the ends of the
earth shall not go on for ever, but only until its climax at the
coming of Jesus. A suggestion is given: this climax is not far
away, according to Luke, who knows that the word continues to
grow and spread (Acts 6:7; 12:24). There is a time-limit for the
preaching, but no fixed time-reference is given. In the last two
references (Acts 10:41–3 and 17:30f.), the parousia has to do
with the last judgement. The speech of Paul on the Areopagus
ends not with the proclamation of the gospel, as in the speeches
to Jews, but with a reference to the judgement day (17:31); the
Gentile world has lived in ignorance, but the time of ignorance
is now over as God has fixed a day for the judgement of the
world. Here Jesus is not the saviour, but the judge, and God has
given the proof of this by raising Jesus from the dead. The line
of thought runs from the resurrection to the judgement, which
shows that the resurrection as such is an eschatological event
ending in the consummation, which here is judgement. So also
in Acts 10:42 the resurrection points forward to Jesus as the
judge of the living and the dead, but here the addressees are
Jews and forgiveness of sins is available (10:43); clearly even the
forgiveness of sins for the people is an eschatological event. No
date for the judgement is given, but in 17:30f. the clear hint is
that it is imminent.[238] When the church proclaims the resurrection it signals that the eschatological drama has begun and is
near its consummation.

Luke does not in Acts lay emphasis upon eschatology. The

---

[237] So H. Conzelmann, *Acts*, 7; E. Grässer, 'Die Parusieerwartung in der Apostel-
      geschichte', in J. Kremer (ed.), *Les Actes des Apôtres*, 115f.; E. Haenchen, *Acts*, 149–52.
[238] R. Maddox, *Purpose*, 130; A.J. Matill, Jr., *Luke and the Last Things*, 43ff.

very fact that the church lives in the end of times and awaits the consummation in the near future is simply a *conditio sine qua non*. And so Luke gives no discourses on eschatology as such; it is never a theme in its own right. In the only speech given to the church in Acts, Paul's farewell speech (20:18–35), not a word is given on the consummation. Eschatology is not a theme in all the speeches, sometimes it is not even touched upon (e.g. Acts 4:8ff.; 7:2–53; 14:14ff.; 17:16ff.), but it is there in all the missionary speeches to the Jews. When dealing with eschatology, the point is not primarily to look forward to what will happen or give a lesson on this. A real problem, however, is the question of the right of admission to the kingdom of God. Above all, is the kingdom of Israel actually coming to Israel? Therefore the main thing is the exhortation to repentance (Acts 2:37ff.; 3:19ff.; 13:26ff.,38ff.), and, when repentance is a fact, the exhortation to hold fast to the grace of God and the true Christian life is decisive (2:41ff.; 4:32ff.; 13:43). It is not only the present time as the last time and the future with the consummation which are important to Luke. He has not only eschatological themes in his speeches, but also résumés of the history of Israel as a speech (7:2–53), or as an important part of a missionary speech (13:17–26): this functions as a guarantee for the future consummation, as the history of the people of God demonstrates God's power over history and his faithfulness to his people.

CHAPTER 4

Acts and the New Testament

Acts holds a unique position within the New Testament. It contains 14 per cent of the New Testament, and, including the Gospel, Luke is responsible for 28 per cent. Acts has no direct literary link with any other New Testament writing. This is clear from its literary genre: Acts is the only example of historiography.[1] Its pattern lies above all in biblical historiography; Luke wrote his history as a part of the biblical history. Acts is stamped with historical and theological views. Stylistically, Acts is unique:[2] Luke has command of a style of 'dramatic episodes'; he is not interested in the episodes as such, but in the continuous historical course, and creates history from histories. He employs in his history-writing a great variety of stylistic means: missionary and apologetic speeches, technical exegesis, erudite expositions, historical résumés, miracle stories, legends, dialogues, prayers, letters, we-passages, sea voyages, summaries, notes, visions, auditions, dreams.

Luke is the only historian among the New Testament authors, writing history on a large scale. From other writings in the New Testament, e.g. from the Gospels and the letters, it is possible to extract historical evidence by the means of deduction from the information present and reconstruction of what actually happened. Luke, however, presents a coherent exposition, where the course of history is theologically decisive. The

[1] Acts has been ascribed to various forms of narrative prose: historiography, respectively historical monograph or apologetical historiography, apocryphal acts, biography, travelogue, praxeis-literature and novel. The majority of scholars see Acts as historiography.

[2] Some scholars find Acts' literary form so special that it is understood as a genre *sui generis*, not representing any form of narrative prose in antiquity.

history of the church is to Luke a part of the history of Israel, continuing in the church as the Israel in the end of times.[3] Luke's contribution in that respect is twofold: the history as such is theologically constituted, and, it would not be possible to know the history of early Christianity at all without Acts, for we would lack too many decisive data.

Before Acts Luke had written a Gospel (Acts 1:1).[4] He was familiar with several Gospels (Luke 1:1–4), among them Mark. As Luke felt the need to write another and better Gospel, because he did not find the ones he knew completely suitable for his purposes, he had to write the continuation of the Gospel in order to bring the account of the history of the people of God to completion. No one had undertaken the same task. There are resonances from the Gospel of Luke in Acts, and echoes, however faint, from other New Testament writings. Some of them regard as more or less distinct the acknowledgement of Jesus as the Messiah and Lord and the destiny of the chosen people. Many of them reflect milieux in which Jewish Christians have an important moulding influence – a distinctive mark of their Christianity is their unwillingness to separate Christianity from the destiny of Israel. The question about the Christian opinion of Israel and its fate was raised again, and again connected with christology as well as ecclesiology. The question about the people of God was the burning question which concerned the 'identity' of the church.

The answers to this question differ. Some of the characters encountered and events narrated in Acts we find also in the letters of *Paul*; there is agreement, but also differences. The apostle to the Gentiles of Paul's letters is, in Acts, the missionary to the Jews. This and other differences have to do with different answers to the question about Israel and the people of God.

---

[3] Luke is not interested in world history at all, and relates the Christ-event only to the history of Israel and to persons and institutions of his own time, cf. H. Conzelmann, *Acts*, xlviif.

[4] I cannot follow the tendency to speak of 'Luke–Acts' as a single book that was later divided and existed in two volumes, so H.J. Cadbury, *The Making of Luke–Acts*; Acts is a literary genre other than the Gospel, it was written several years later, is dealing with other themes, has other theological ideas and corresponds to the largest size of a standard scroll, so that the Gospel and Acts as one book would be technically far too large.

Luke's original ideas about the divided people of God, the indictment of the unrepentant and the church as the restored Israel are not the same as Paul's. In Paul's former letters he separates Christianity from Israel. He makes a very bitter indictment of the Jews: the wrath of God has definitively fallen upon them (1 Thess. 2:14–16); circumcision is mutilation, all Jewish prerogatives are written off, as is Israel as a whole (Phil. 3:2ff.; Gal. 6:15); there is neither Jew not Greek, but a new 'race' and a new creation, the only persons of faith are the children of Abraham (Gal. 3:16ff.,28; 6:15f.). In Romans, however, we have a different attitude: Israel has not been rejected; the unholy, ungodly and unrepentant Israel is forever the people of God and the children of Abraham (Rom. 9–11; further Rom. 3:1ff.; 4:1,12–16; 7:7ff.; 8:4); a minor part of Israel is already saved and constitutes the centre of the church (Rom. 11:2–5,16–22); to the rest God grants a 'general amnesty', since the whole of Israel, after a temporary rejection, shall be saved at the end of times (Rom. 11:26ff.).

In *Matthew* Jesus is seen as the Lord of the Gentile nations, 'all the nations', with 'all authority in heaven and on earth', and the church is for all the peoples (28:18–20). Israel does not any longer exist as the people of God, but has been replaced by another people, coming from all the Gentile nations (8:11–12; 21:43; 27:15–26; 28:18–20). The rejection of Israel is the response to Israel's rejection of the Messiah (27:15–26). Still the Jewish Christians can live in the church with the best conscience, because the heritage of Israel, the Messiah and the law of Moses can be found there (5–7; 23:1ff.). In the Gospel of *John* the Jews represent 'the world' in its hostility towards God[5] *and* the world in its faith in God. The coming of Jesus meant his revelation to Israel (1:31); Jesus is the 'king of Israel' (1:49; 12:13), the disciple the true Israelite (1:47); salvation comes from the Jews (4:22), and Jesus dies for Israel (18:14). The believers are being banned from the synagogue (9:22; 12:42; 16:2). With Jesus the judgement comes, and Israel is divided (3:18ff.; 7:43; 9:16; 10:19): there have always been two groups in the people of

---

[5]   R. Bultmann, *Theology of the New Testament* II, London 1955, 15ff.,26ff.; *The Gospel of John*, Oxford 1971, Index: 'Judaism'.

Israel, the one 'of the truth' and the other doing evil and speaking lies (3:20,21; 8:23,44,47; 10:26,27; 17:6,9,14), and through the coming of Jesus-Messiah these groups were separated. Only the one group is and has ever been Israel, and this group is the church, whereas the non-believing part of Israel has never belonged to Israel (5:36–47; 8:30–59). Israel has not been rejected for a new people, but lives on in the church.

In these writings the question about Israel is elaborated and of actual importance for the readers. In other writings the question is touched upon, but the ideas are there in the background for the authors.

In *Hebrews* the question about Israel plays an important role, however indirectly. The actual topics and themes, e.g. the question of the law, Moses, ceremonies, the sanctuary, are dealt with in a highly original and independent way. The letter is written to Jewish Christians[6] in order to prevent a relapse into Judaism (10:25,29; 13:9–14). The Gentiles are not even mentioned. The church is 'the people', a term used equally of Israel and the church (2:17; 4:9; 5:3; 7:5,11,27; 10:30; 13:12). The church is also called 'meeting', *episynagogē*, (10:25), understood as the continuation of the synagogue, and 'the house', the one house throughout the history of the people (3:2,6; 10:21). There is no replacement of the old people. Jesus took to himself the 'seed of Abraham' (2:16),[7] and he died for Israel (2:16; 13:12). The church is the 'pilgrim people', and represents a new relationship between God and Israel. The law was inadequate, a shadow and subject to changes (7:11,12,16,19; 10:1ff.), and the sacrificial system and the old covenant obsolete, superseded by a new high priest and a new covenant (7–10). There is a division within Israel,[8] but this is understood so that former generations in Israel did not find salvation (2:1ff.; 4:1ff.; 10:39), even if faith always was the mark of Israel (3:16ff.; 11:1ff.). So Israel has found salvation and its history continues in the church.

In the *Revelation* 'Jew' is an honorary name (2:9; 3:9), meant as a designation for the Christian. The Jews from the synagogue

---

[6] Cf. B. Lindars, *The Theology of the Letter to the Hebrews*, NTT, Cambridge 1991, 4–15.
[7] This term used for Israel: Luke 1:55; Acts 7:5f.; Gal. 3:16; 2 Cor. 11:22.
[8] But different from that in both Luke and John.

are lying when claiming to be 'Jews' (3:9), and their synagogue is Satan's (2:9; 3:9). These persons are unbelieving Jews, but the true Jews are the Christians. This is not understood as an honorary name regardless of the ethnic background, and this is clear from the great scene with the vision of the heavenly church at the end of times (7:4–17): there are two groups in the church, namely the 144,000 from the twelve tribes of Israel (7:4–8) and an innumerable amount from all the nations (7:9–10). Thus the the fate of Israel is seen as the salvation of a remnant of the people.

The various solutions to the question about Israel determine even central theological topics and themes in the New Testament writings. That Gentiles will participate in the kingdom of God is common, as is the principle 'for the Jews first', but there are great differences in the theological basis. Luke saw the Gentile mission as God's commandment in Scripture, a part of the promises to Israel, and an appendix to the mission to the Jews. This mission to the Jews was completed by Paul. Israel is restored. For *Paul* himself the 'righteousness without the law' meant that God was the God even of the Gentiles and had broken down 'the middle wall of partition', the law, between Jews and Gentiles. The mission to the Gentiles and their 'fullness' has as its outcome the salvation of all Israel. In *Matthew* the life and work of Jesus was God's mission to his people: when Israel rejected Messiah and his gospel, God rejected his people and, through the death of Christ, substituted for it a church of the nations. The commandment to Gentile mission is given after this rejection (Matt. 28:18–20). In the Gospel of *John* the salvation of Gentiles has only a shadowy life, mentioned explicitly in 12:20ff., and twice when talking about 'sheep not belonging to this fold' (John 10:16; 11:52, cf. 7:35). There is no specific commandment for the Gentile mission. John's interest is focused on the Jews inside and outside the church: the principle 'for the Jews first' is the dominant theme in Jesus' earthly ministry to Israel, but there is a universal mission after the mission to the Jews has come to an end, and the believers are gathered, because the historical and geographical limitations are dissolved by his death (12:20–32). Jesus' death and ascension to the Father inaugurate the Gentile mission. The Gentiles[9] come as an addition to 'the flock', Israel (10:16).[10]

The ideas about Israel and mission bear upon the concept of the law. Luke treats the law as decisive for ecclesiology.[11] *Paul*, within a different anthropology, places the law foremost within soteriology: Christ is the end to the law in contrast with faith. The law as a temporary measure was intended to bring consciousness of sin and set the world, Jews and Gentiles alike, under God's judgement and wrath (Rom. 3:19–31; 7:7–25; 10:4; Gal. 3:1–29). *Matthew* has a harsh polemic against the pharisaic interpretation of the law (Matt. 5:20–46); Jesus interprets the law with divine authority as the 'exceeding righteousness', revealing the true will of God. The whole law is summarized as love for God and the neighbour (7:12; 22:37–40); every single commandment in the law requires love of God and charity to others. Matthew sees the law as a part of ecclesiology: the true people of God is the 'nation that yields the proper fruit' (21:43; 28:20) and which lives according to Jesus' interpretation of the law. The *Fourth Gospel* sees the law in terms of christology. Moses is a witness to Christ (John 1:45; 5:46); therefore the Mosaic law is a testimony, whereas Jesus is the reality to which Moses testified (1:17); the law accuses the Jews when they oppose Jesus (5:45; 7:19ff.; 10:34). As testimony the law is provisional and superseded by the fulfilment in Christ. The letter to the *Hebrews* sets the law in the frame of christology. The law is a shadow of the things to come in Christ (Heb. 10:1ff.; 7:11–19), and therefore after his coming is inadequate and inferior.

A crucial area in the development of New Testament theology is christology and above all the understanding of the death of Christ. Luke's contribution lies foremost in his presentation of Jesus as the most Jewish Messiah within the New Testament: he is the Messiah of Israel and only in this capacity the Lord over the world. Another important contribution is the

---

[9] Are 'the Greeks' of the Fourth Gospel proselytes or God-fearers?
[10] This is not far from the Lucan ideas (Acts 15:13ff.) about Israel and a people of Gentiles 'for his name'.
[11] See the section 'The law', in chapter three above.

notion of Jesus as a man, but in a defined historical context:
Jesus is a Jewish man, who falls into line with the history of the
people. All New Testament writers presuppose that Jesus died
for our sins, but understand this in various ways. For *Matthew*
the passion means the rejection of Israel and the birth of the
church through the forgiveness of sins. *John* sees his death as
the exaltation of Jesus to divine glory and the demonstration of
the total unity between Jesus and God, by means of which the
believer is brought into union with God. For *Paul* the death
of Jesus is atonement and reconciliation, in that Jesus bore the
guilt of the world on the cross and broke down the power of sin.
In *Revelation* the death means a cosmic victory: the power of
Satan is broken. In *Hebrews* the death of Jesus inaugurates the
new covenant as the final and all-sufficient atonement sacrifice
with permanent efficacy.

Luke has his own contribution. He combines the diverse
viewpoints of the writings of the New Testament, not as
historian or compiler, but as theologian. It is not only the death
of Jesus which is seen as the salvation from sins, but rather the
whole of Jesus' life and work: life, death, resurrection, ascension
and parousia. These acts combined mean redemption. Luke
acknowledges the sacrificial death of Jesus and thrusts it into the
background, but the crucial point is the connection of two
aspects: the Jews killed Jesus and his death was God's will, a
divine 'necessity'.

CHAPTER 5

Acts in the history of early Christianity

The contribution of Acts to our knowledge of the history of early Christianity is invaluable. First, Luke gives us information about what happened in the church from its beginnings to the last decade of the first century. Second, Acts itself is a testimony to the role of Jewish Christianity in the last decades of the first century and then furnishes us with a concept of the whole church. This has to do with the Jewishness of Acts in christology, ecclesiology, soteriology, the question of the law, the language – namely biblical Greek – and the portrait of Paul. Luke's interest in Jews and Jewish Christians is obvious. The explanation of this Jewishness, however, involves even the composition of the Lucan community. The catchword for this explanation is 'history'; all the Jewish elements belong, for Luke, to the past. The time of Jesus belongs to the past, so do the apostolic era and the time of Paul, and Luke's own time is that of the third generation. Luke is a Gentile Christian, representing Gentile Christianity at the end of the century.

The common conception of early Christianity is by and large accepted: Christianity was in the beginning (Palestinian) Jewish Christianity; in the second period we find side by side Hellenistic Jewish Christianity, Gentile Hellenistic Christianity and Paul; in the third – when Luke lived – Gentile Christianity triumphed. In the second period, after 48 AD, Jewish Christianity was forced back and acted solely on the defensive, while in the third period, after 70 AD, Jewish Christianity mostly disappeared. Jewish Christians returned to the synagogue, became Gentile Christians, or settled as isolated Christian-

Jewish sects. This last phenomenon later became 'Jewish Christianity'.

Luke does not represent the triumphant Gentile Christianity of after 70 AD. He is surely a historian, but he does not write history only to preserve records for posterity. He writes about his own time in order to understand the apparently familiar phenomena, recalling what has happened and what happens as binding on the life of his own church. He considers the past as the ideal time of the church and as a norm. The history *per se* is not essential, but the significance of history is; as it was in the beginning of the time of the church, it shall be even today. That means that Luke's own church is a Jewish-Christian church. Jewish Christianity from the beginning was a multifarious phenomenon. A single Jewish Christianity never existed, only a great diversity of theological conceptions and groups resting on the common denominator Jewish Christianity, which resisted the separation of Christianity from the religious, political and cultural fate of Israel.

Acts tells us that Jewish Christianity was an important and diverse part of the church throughout the first century, at least equal to Gentile Christianity.[1] Jewish Christianity was not marginal, but in the mainstream of the church even after 70 AD. The Jewish Christians did not become Gentile Christians, and they saw themselves as the centre of the church. Luke is our most important witness to this fact. The dominant role of Jewish Christianity from 30 AD to the Apostolic Council is clear, and its growing strength is seen in the bitter fight over the question of the legitimacy of the mission to the Gentiles in the first period of the church. The witnesses to this are Paul, the Synoptic Gospels and Acts. After the Apostolic Council Jewish Christianity played an important role: this is confirmed above all by the theologian of Gentile Christianity *par excellence*, Paul, himself a Jewish Christian, or becoming more of one in the last period of his work. The importance of the Jewish group can be seen from the successful Jewish-Christian anti-Pauline propaganda in the Pauline missionary field, which we can follow

---

[1]   'Equal' does not refer to numbers, but to theological influence and importance.

above all in his last letters. Jewish Christians in Jerusalem adopted a harder line than Paul's law-free mission among the Gentiles after the Apostolic Council. The Jewish-Christian influence forced Paul into a reorientation and extension of his theology and thinking. Until the letter to the Romans Paul separated Christianity from the destiny of Israel. In Romans the destiny of Israel and the Jews is still an open one. In Romans 9–11 Paul works up in a positive way the destiny of Israel as part of his preaching of the righteousness of God;[2] a minor part of Israel constitutes the centre of the church (11:2–6,16–22). The saying ' to the Jews first and also to the Greeks' we have only in Romans (1:17; 2:10). Israel is forever the people of God.

After the death of Paul Jewish Christianity had a dominant place in the church. The authority of the church in Jerusalem is not questioned. The Jewish Christians lived as numerical minorities in the churches outside Palestine, but theologically and culturally as 'mighty minorities', constantly setting the agenda of the church. Jews and Gentiles lived together as distinct groups, as a look at the Pauline churches and Acts shows. In the years 70–100 we find a most lively discussion of how the mission to the Gentiles can be justified. The *Sitz im Leben* for this discussion is what happened to the Jewish Christians after they had to live in Gentile surroundings, separated and isolated from their own people, still claiming to be Israel. Before the year 70 AD Jewish Christians belonged just as much to the church as to the synagogue, but now they are separated more and more from their people. The synagogues exclude them, and they live as minorities in a milieu with non-Jews. How can Gentiles and heathens become a majority in Israel? Not all Jewish Christians continued to live in the church. Some left and joined the synagogue again; others lived in isolation in the church and became Christian sects. A significant number, however, lived together with Gentile Christians.

Our main witness to the role those groups played is Acts. Luke falls into line with the Jewish-Christian parts of Paul's teaching.[3] Luke is not our only witness – other writings from

---

[2] J. Jervell, *Unknown Paul*, 34ff.

[3] The other line from Paul can be found in the Pastoral letters and 1 Peter.

the same period, such as the Gospels of Matthew and John, the
letter to the Hebrews and the Revelation, reveal the diversity
of Jewish-Christian influence in the last decades of the
century,[4] but the most important contribution comes from
Acts. What does the church look like, how it is made up and
what is its way of thinking at the end of Acts? Where has 'the
way' from Jerusalem to Rome led the church? The composition of the church in Luke's time would not have been very
different from the one Luke describes in Acts. It is commonly
held that the Jewish influence in the church, at least from a
literary point of view, reached its climax in the third generation
of Christians in the first century.[5] This would not be possible
without a considerable number of Jews in the church. Acts
does not describe the whole church; it is the church in Palestine
and the Roman Empire. There is nothing like an established
and uniform church. The group behind the church in Acts is
other than that we have behind the Gospel of John, Revelation, Hebrews and the Pastorals. The church of Acts had a
considerable number of Jews and some Gentiles, and the
Gentiles have to adjust to the Jews, not the other way round. It
is different, for example, in the Pastorals, where the Jews have
to adjust to the Gentiles, becoming Gentile Christians, in order
to be accepted. As a whole, however, it was possible for Jews
and Gentiles to live together. The theology is Jewish-Christian
within a church headed by the church in Jerusalem. This
church is, for the most part, the outcome of Paul's work. It is
not the only Pauline church, as we have a different group
behind the Pastoral letters, in which the church members, with
some exceptions, are Gentiles, and both churches live on the
Pauline missionary territory. There are different solutions to
the question about the fate of Israel. Acts represents the idea
that the church, thanks to the Jewish element, is to be understood as the true continuation of Israel: the church has not
separated itself from Israel, but is obviously separated from

---

[4]   See J. Jervell, *Unknown Paul*, 43–50.
[5]   E.g., H. Conzelmann, 'Heidenchristentum', *RGG* III, 141; L. Goppelt, *Christentum
       und Judentum im ersten und zweiten Jahrhundert*, Gütersloh 1954, 149f.; B. Reicke, *The
       New Testament Era*, Philadelphia 1968, 291f.

the synagogue. The solution represented by Paul, that the salvation of all Israel is the goal in the way God deals with the salvation of the Gentiles and the world, is given up.

There is obviously no great zeal for a mission among Jews, something which is partly understood in Acts: the mission among Jews is ended, as the work is done all over the Dispersion. The church has definitely turned to the Gentiles. Eschatology is not a burning issue any more, even if we find a flourishing of the expectation that the parousia is near at hand.

We usually say that the New Testament is a document of Gentile Christianity. This is true when it comes to the collection of writings, the canon, but it is not true when we are dealing with the coming into existence of the individual documents in the New Testament. This history is not written by the victor, because a great deal of the writings, and the most influential ones, show the influence and power of Jewish Christianity. And in the front rank we find Luke's Acts.

CHAPTER 6

The significance of Acts for today

The modern study of Acts has been occupied with the question of the original setting and meaning of the document. Is it possible, in this document from the first century, to find any contemporary significance, that is apart from the significance every historical document has as a witness to history as such? The question about contemporary significance concerns whether Acts has any place in contemporary theology and preaching, apart from as a part of our Christian inheritance, or whether the arguments of the author are completely locked in the presuppositions of the past? Certainly, all of the theological arguments are determined by the world in the first Christian century. Still some of the basic theological thoughts transcend the first century. It is out of the question to attempt to apply contemporary significance to the whole of Acts for the modern reader, at least for those who read the New Testament for spiritual profit, but when making such an application the *conditio sine qua non* is that our contemporary interpretation must be true to the original meaning. There are two addressees for this contemporary significance: the church, and the world to which the church addresses its message.

Acts has never felt alien to the readers, thanks to Luke's great skill as narrator. Our picture of the history of the early church comes in largest measure from Luke: even Paul's own letters have been far less influential than Acts in enabling readers to gain an understanding of his life and work. Luke's history of the church, built up in episodes and stories, is easily accessible to modern readers. But this way of writing history has its weaknesses: to some extent it hands over the interpretation of the stories to the readers' different interpretations, which become somewhat remote from the intentions Luke had. A different matter is the question of whether the theological presuppositions behind Acts have significance for today. To come to grips with these we should read Acts imaginatively, trying to enter the situation of the readers and feel Luke's anxiety and responsibility for them. Luke is anything but a neutral observer, and Acts is not a general historical treatise, but addressed to particular people doubtful of their right to be the people of God. Luke therefore writes history as an attempt to solve the problems of his church, not addressing the church as a whole, but one particular group of people in a situation very different from ours.

The girder in Luke's theological thinking is the notion of *God* being in complete control of history. God is the active force in history, almighty throughout the course of history, so that it is impossible for men to resist his will, at least in the long run. In the words of Gamaliel, 'For if this idea of theirs [i.e. the Christians] or its execution is of human origin, it will collapse; but if it is from God, you will never be able to put them down, and you risk finding yourselves at war with God' (Acts 5:37f.). Compared to God, humans act like puppets. History as such has a meaning and a plan, for it is filled with God's saving acts. This seems strange to our modern idea of history in two ways: we find no meaning in the historical process and reckon only with man as the active and creative force. It is still fully valid to see God as involved in history and even in control of history, but the question is in what way? For the church it is not history as such which is decisive, but the sense of history; the idea that man is in control of history and himself has collapsed. This is seen above all from the fact that historically we achieve the opposite of what we aim at. The historical process is full of surprises and enigmas, to which we have no explanations. This does not mean that we put God in the inexplicable facts of the historical process, but that we understand his involvement above all from an ethical and eschatological point of view. It is possible to see in many historical events where God's will is

fulfilled and where 'we are at war with God'. Humans always
act in some sort of apprehension of God – or, some would
prefer to say, of life – and the human apprehension of God is
another side of God's self-revelation. So the outcome of the
historical process will be salvation and liberation of humanity,
as the result not of some kind of development, but of God's
creative act and intervention.

This means that we can see parts of the Lucan understanding
of God's involvement in history as of contemporary significance. Which, at the same time, means that we put parts of
Acts *ad acta*. We cannot reiterate the notion of God as the God
of Israel and not of the nations, not the interpretation that
God's involvement in history is restricted to the history of the
chosen people with almost no concern for the history of the
nations or the world as a whole. We can even cross out the idea
that the church is Israel, a meaningful notion only when the
members of the church are themselves Jews coming from the
synagogue. This was replaced in the second century by the idea
of the church as the new Israel, where the church members
were neither Jews nor Gentiles, but looked upon themselves as
'tertium genus', 'the third nation'. On the other hand, it is an
undisputable fact that the prehistory of the church is the history
of Israel, and that the heritage of Israel still is a significant part
of the church's faith. That implies that the church has a clear
responsibility for the fate of Israel, that is the religion of Israel.

The church of Luke consisted of Jews and non-Jews. There
were great problems attached to the fellowship and life together
of the two groups, problems known to us from nearly all the
communities described in the New Testament. They are com-
prehensible because of the understanding Jews had of their own
identity in relation to 'the nations', which enforced distance and
separatism. On the other hand, the Gentiles had problems in
joining a national–religious group like the Jews. Luke's solution
to this problem is the Apostolic Decree: Jews are not forced to
give up their distinctive stamp as Jews, and the Gentiles do not
have to become Jews or like Jews in order to live in fellowship
in this church of Jewish origin. The Gentiles had to adjust to
some Jewish laws, but never became Jews; they had to give up

practices connected with their former religion – which the church understood as idolatry – but remained non-Jews. Our problems in the church of today in this field are not the relations between Jews and Gentiles, but those between different groups coming from various nations, cultures, political backgrounds etc. What Luke achieved in keeping the groups together in fellowship without any effort to remove their distinctive stamp, e.g. cultural, national, is still of great significance.

Luke's *christology* is shaped by the idea of Jesus as the Messiah of Israel. The specific claim is that the revelation of God and his acts in the history of Israel, and thereby in history as a whole, reaches its climax in Jesus. The various titles of Jesus, all of Jewish origin, attempt to consolidate this claim. When Luke refers to the gospel being preached in non-Jewish surroundings, he does not replace the Jewish titles with others more intelligible for non-Jews. The titles are combined with a series of colourful stories and parables about Jesus' words and works. These stories are irreplaceable, but the situation is different with the titles. Even if those titles have only historical value for us, Luke's way of creating christology still has contemporary significance. It is impossible simply to dispose of titles and to form christology only by telling stories about the work of Christ. The stories are indispensable even today in the formation of christology, but not sufficient on their own. The accumulation and great variety of titles to be found in Luke–Acts gives the church the freedom and obligation to find new titles in order to show the identity of Christ, his influence throughout history and his contemporary identity and role. Furthermore, as the titles were chosen from the social, cultural and religious milieu of the first Christians, we should today take titles from our own various milieux. If by doing this we end up with a variety of titles, some of them limited to various cultures, we can only enrich christology. The principle of a variety of titles of different origins is well known to early Christianity. A characteristic of Lucan christology – this goes for both the Gospel and Acts – is the absence of titles revealing a background of metaphysical speculation. Jesus is depicted above all with human qualities; he is subordinate to God; he is simply a man in history, or *the* man, in a unique historic position. But in this man God reveals himself to the world once and for all.

The way the *Scriptures* are used is most alien to readers of today. The Old Testament is treated as the word of God, the whole of it and every single word. Everything has absolute authority, even if Luke especially refers to specific parts, above all the prophets and the psalms. At every stage of Luke's argument he invokes Scripture. A citation is regarded as conclusive proof, and this is so even with regard to the question of the resurrection of Jesus (Acts 2:25ff.; 13:34ff., cf. Luke 18:31–4). Prophecies of the future are taken to apply to Jesus as the Messiah of God. Luke tries to strengthen this argument by demonstrating that even in the history of Israel before Christ God fulfilled promises given in Scripture. There is not the slightest hint of any criticism of any part of Scripture, in spite of Luke's following what he considers to be the literal meaning of the Scripture, which he does in a very logical and rational way. There is nothing esoteric about Scripture. No part of Scripture is held to be inadequate and obsolete. So, for example, all the laws of the Pentateuch, even the ritual and ceremonial ones, are not superseded, but fully valid and therefore to be kept by the church, that is by its Jewish members. Luke employs the Scriptures in this specific way because in the actual situation of his readers nothing else will satisfy, and create the necessary certainty in, their faith and identity as the people of God. This goes both for the members of the church and for those this church addressed in its missionary efforts. Therefore the promises of God as well as their fulfilment, the patterns for christology and church, the mission to non-Jews and the laws to be followed, everything must have scriptural proof.

It is impossible for us to assume today Luke's use of the Old Testament and his scriptural proofs. From that angle you can convince nobody about the Christian truth. The Old Testament is not a frame of reference for the people the church addresses or even for the people in the church. Still, Luke's ideas on this point have contemporary significance. The Old Testament is indispensable for the church, for more than historical reasons. The testimony of the Old Testament about God and his works and his dealing with the world and mankind is the pattern for our understanding and confession of God: the Old Testament, however, must be interpreted critically. The Old Testament is not a Christian book, but a book in its own right, the book of Israel; as such it is only one part of the prehistory of the Christian faith and church, and opens up the possibility of other sources in history being seen as the word of God. The laws in the Old Testament, critically interpreted, retain their value as a source for moral instruction, seen not as a specific Christian ethic, only applying to Christians, but as being for all humans. Third, it is necessary for the church to have some frame of reference common to all men and women alike, making it possible to argue for the Christian faith from what seems to be rational, with the way Luke saw the Old Testament as a pattern.

There is, however, not much rationality in the way Acts describes the *Spirit*. The Spirit is an impersonal and dynamic force, God's creative presence in the church, visible and manifesting itself in miracles, wonders, glossolalia, inspiration, visions, auditions and, above all, in prophetic sayings. The Spirit legitimates the church, as these charismatic phenomena are comprehended as proofs that the church is God's creation and that God alone guides and rules his people. The story of the gospel 'from Jerusalem to Rome' is the story of God with particular people, and the subject of this history is 'the Holy Spirit and us'. It is the *raison d'être* for the church in that it is more than a human organization, and so a creation of God and an instrument for the proclamation of the gospel. This part of Lucan ecclesiology is still of the utmost significance. Another question is the way Luke comprehends the essence and activity of the Spirit. Even if there has been a revival of the charismatic in some (established) churches in the last years these phenomena cannot be regarded as any kind of proof for the divine character of the church, not least as they are known from many religions, and not even reserved for religions. In his comprehension of the Spirit Luke is far behind the depths in Paul's understanding, which is of far greater contemporary

significance. Most important for us today is Luke's combination of Spirit and prophecy, that is the ability of the church to
interpret history, world, time and events theologically, in their
relation to God and future.

The gospel is being preached 'from Jerusalem to Rome', that
is in the Roman Empire. Owing to that Luke has to deal with
the *political powers* of his time, that is the relation between
church and the Roman Empire. He has no theological definition, interpretation or evaluation of Empire and state, but
simply recognizes the existence of Rome as a political reality.
The inferiority of the state compared to God is seen, as the
political power in some cases is forced to serve God's purposes,
that is to spread the gospel in the Empire and to Rome. Luke
describes the freedom of the church towards the Empire, a
freedom determined by the church's task to proclaim the
gospel. The only defiance of the political authorities comes
when faced with their attempts to hamper the preaching of the
gospel, and so the practical behaviour of the church is seen: no
subversion or defiance. The church is politically harmless, no
threat to the state. This attitude has its basis in Luke's
eschatology: the kingdom will replace the Empire anyway. This
attitude of Luke has some contemporary significance: it is still
the main task for the church to preach the gospel and to defy
any hindrances to this, and the church as such has no political
programme, but the gospel has implications of a social and
cultural and political sort, and Luke considered those implications would be realized eschatologically, that is in the kingdom
of God, and proleptically in the inner life and fellowship of the
Christian community. As we have other ideas about eschatology
the consequence is a political and social activity from the
church, where this is possible; that is, under other circumstances
Luke's guidelines are still valid.

When Luke deals with the problem of the identity of the
church and the legitimacy of its gospel he turns to history,
God's history with his people, where the justification for the
church's existence is given; the catchword is 'from of old'. But
history has not so far reached its consummation. Here we face
eschatology. Eschatology is not a substitute for a meaningless and

tragic history or the answer to a crisis in the church, e.g. the delay of the parousia. But as history is God's history there has to be a terminal point and a consummation, which means the kingdom of God. This is clear from Scripture. Luke is fully aware of the situation of the church: it lives in the end of times, God's plan for the ultimate and last saving act, that in Christ, is on the brink of completion. Luke is fully aware of the fact that there has been a delay of the parousia. He gives no reason for this and does not seem to see it as a problem; he simply asserts that the end of times has come and that even in the endtime there is a time interval, though obviously a short one. There is a clear 'now and not yet' dialectic in his way of thinking.

It is hard for our 'modern understanding' to come to grips with the eschatology of Acts. It is not difficult to grasp what Luke has to say, but it is hard to agree with the argument as we do not share his presuppositions. We do not see God as the active force in history in the way Luke did and therefore we find no meaning, no plan and no aim, no end. We are fully aware of the possibility of a disaster, a catastrophe which could mean the end of the world, but this is not the same as the idea in Acts of the kingdom of God. On the contrary it has nothing to do with God at all: the possible disaster is the achievement of men, and there is no hope for the future connected with it. In spite of this the message of Acts has contemporary significance. First, as eschatology is connected with Jesus: he is the ultimate 'word' of God, the last thing about God and humanity has been said; no more messages about salvation will come. Second, there is a common frame of reference in the experiences of the fear of possible disasters and threats to our world, even as the result of human acts: namely these conceived of as judgements. In confronting these with the message of Acts, we may turn fear into hope. Third, the human apprehension of God is an apprehension of something fragmentary, partial, uncompleted. When will it be whole?

Acts as a whole leaves us with a desideratum: to write a *Geschichtstheologie*, a theology of history. In Acts, Luke has given us the pattern in writing the history of the church in the world-wide context of general history, that is the Roman Empire. The church has not come to an end: history goes on, and this history must be written. But no one undertakes today to give us a theological interpretation of the history of the church within history. Theology of history has deserted the field and handed it over to the *Geschichtsphilosophie*, philosophy of history. Is the reason that such an undertaking is not possible anymore? If so: why not?

Select bibliography

COMMENTARIES

The following represents the most influential commentaries in the last forty years with a radical–critical approach (Conzelmann, Haenchen), older commentaries from critical schools (Overbeck, Lake/Cadbury), one older and some of the more recent conservative approaches (Bruce, Marshall), and a selection of the most recent commentaries (Pesch, Schneider, Roloff).

Barrett, C.K., *The Acts of the Apostles* I, International Critical Commentary, Edinburgh 1994

Bruce, F.F., *The Acts of the Apostles*, Grand Rapids [3] 1990

Conzelmann, H., *Acts of the Apostles*, Hermeneia, Philadelphia 1987 (translated from German: *Die Apostelgeschichte*, Göttingen [2] 1972)

Haenchen, E., *The Acts of the Apostles*, Oxford 1971 (translated from German: *Die Apostelgeschichte*, KEK, Göttingen[14] 1965)

Lake, K., and Cadbury, H.J., *The Acts of the Apostles*, Beg. IV, V, London 1933

Marshall, I.H., *Acts. An Introduction and Commentary*, TNTC, Leicester 1980

Overbeck, F., *Kurze Erklärung der Apostelgeschichte, Kurzgefas. exeg. Handbuch zum Neuen Testament von W.L.M. de Wette* I/4, Leipzig [4] 1870

Pesch, R., *Die Apostelgeschichte*, EKK V/1–2, Neukirchen 1986

Roloff, J., *Die Apostelgeschichte*, NTD 5, Göttingen [2] 1988

Schneider, G., *Die Apostelgeschichte* I–II, HThK V/1, Freiburg/Basle/Vienna 1980, 1982

GENERAL STUDIES

Systematic studies of the theology of Acts are rare after Conzelmann, but the following general studies and surveys over the research will be found useful:

Barrett, C.K., *Luke the Historian in Recent Study*, London 1961

Bovon, F., *Luke the Theologian: Thirty-Three Years of Research*, Allison Park, PA, 1987

Cadbury, H.J., *The Making of Luke–Acts*, New York 1927

Conzelmann, H., *The Theology of St Luke*, London 1960 (translated from German: *Die Mitte der Zeit*, BHTh 17, Tübingen 1954)

Dibelius, M., *Studies in the Acts of the Apostles*, London 1956 (translated from German: *Aufsätze zur Apostelgeschichte*, FRLANT 60, Göttingen 1951)

Fitzmyer, J.A., *Luke the Theologian: Aspects of His Teaching*, New York 1990

Foakes-Jackson, F.J., and Lake, K. (eds.), *The Beginnings of Christianity* I, *The Acts of the Apostles* I–V, London 1920–33

Franklin, E., *Christ the Lord. A Study in the Purpose and Theology of Luke–Acts*, London 1975

Jervell, J., *Luke and the People of God*, Minneapolis 1972

Jervell, J., *The Unknown Paul*, Minneapolis 1984

Keck, L.E., and Martyn, J.L. (eds.), *Studies in Luke–Acts. Essays Presented in Honor of P. Schubert*, Philadelphia [2] 1980

Kremer, J. (ed.), *Les Actes des Apôtres. Traditions, rédaction, théologie*, BETL 48, Leuven 1979

Lohfink, G., *Die Sammlung Israels. Eine Untersuchung zur lukanischen Ekklesiologie*, StANT 26, Munich 1971

Maddox, R., *The Purpose of Luke–Acts*, FRLANT 126, Göttingen 1982

Marshall, I.H., *Luke, Historian and Theologian*, Exeter/Grand Rapids 1979

SPECIAL STUDIES

Bock, D.L., *Proclamation from Prophecy and Pattern. Lucan Old Testament Christology*, JSNTSS 17, Sheffield 1987

Bovon, F., *L'oeuvre de Luc. Etudes d'exégèse et de théologie*, Lectio Divina 130, Paris 1987

Dahl, N.A, 'A People for His Name', *NTS* 4, 1958, 319–27

Dunn, J.D.G., *Baptism in the Holy Spirit*, London 1970

Dupont, J., *The Salvation of the Gentiles. Essays on the Acts of the Apostles*, New York 1979

Esler, P., *Community and Gospel in Luke–Acts*, Cambridge 1978

George, A., L'esprit saint dans l'oeuvre de Luc', *RB* 85, 1978, 500–42

Klinghardt, M., *Gesetz und Volk Gottes. Das lukanische Verständnis des Gesetzes nach Herkunft, Funktion und seinem Ort in der Geschichte des Urchristentums*, WUNT 32, Tübingen 1988

Lampe, G.H.W., *The Holy Spirit in the Writings of St Luke. Essays in Memory of R.H. Lightfoot*, Oxford 1955, 159–200

Matill, A.J. Jr. *Luke and the Last Things: A Perspective for Understanding of Lukan Thought*, Dillsboro NC 1979

Tajra, H.W., *The Trial of St Paul*, WUNT 35, Tübingen 1989

Thornton, C.-J., *Der Zeuge des Zeugen. Lukas als Historiker der Paulusreisen*, WUNT, 1991

Vielhauer, P. 'The "Paulinism" of the Acts of the Apostles', in Keck, L.E., and Martyn, J.L. (eds.), *Studies in Luke–Acts. Essays Presented in Honor of P. Schubert*, Philadelphia 1980

Index